B

The Restorative Practices Handbook

◆◆

for Teachers, Disciplinarians and Administrators

by
Bob Costello,
Joshua Wachtel
and Ted Wachtel

INTERNATIONAL INSTITUTE FOR RESTORATIVE PRACTICES
Bethlehem, Pennsylvania, USA

THE RESTORATIVE PRACTICES HANDBOOK
FOR TEACHERS, DISCIPLINARIANS AND ADMINISTRATORS
Copyright © 2009
International Institute for Restorative Practices
All Rights Reserved

10
FIRST EDITION
Printed in Canada

INTERNATIONAL INSTITUTE FOR RESTORATIVE PRACTICES
P.O. Box 229
Bethlehem, PA 18016 USA

BOOK AND COVER DESIGN
Christopher MacDonald

COVER PHOTO
Ronnie Andren

Library of Congress Control Number: 2008939654
ISBN-13: 978-1-934355-02-2
ISBN-10: 1-934355-02-X

Table of Contents

Note for Readers Outside the U.S.   vii

INTRODUCTION   New Thinking, New Practice, New Result   1

CHAPTER 1   Restorative Practices in the Classroom   9

     Affective Statements   12

     Affective Questions   16

     Small Impromptu Conferences   21

     Circles   23
        "Check-in"
        "Check-out"
        Classroom Norms
        Classroom Content
        Academic Goals
        Behavior Problems
        Being Proactive
        Some Tips for Running Circles

     Formal Conferences   33
        Restorative Conferences
        Family Group Decision Making

     Overcoming Resistance   38

CHAPTER 2   Restorative Practices and Discipline   43

     Restorative Practices in Conduct   47

     Social Discipline   49

     Fostering Understanding   52

     Repairing the Harm   54

     Apologies   58

     Attending to Needs   59

     Punishment   62

     Active Involvement   64

	The Nine Affects and the Compass of Shame	68
	When Things Go Badly	74
	Consequences	76
CHAPTER 3	**Leadership and School Change**	**79**
	Perceiving the Need for Change	82
	The Vision of Restorative Practices	82
	Organizational Change: A Practical Approach	84
	Organizational Change Window	85

Change TO People
Change FOR People
NOT Doing Change
Change WITH People

	Fair Process	86
	Tips for Working with Staff	88
	Overcoming Teacher Resistance	91
	Getting Students and Parents on Board	94
	Other Applications	95
	Maintaining Momentum and the Need for Self-Assessment	96
	Conclusion	98

References	**99**
Educational Resources	**103**
About the IIRP	**109**
Restorative Works Learning Network	**110**
About the Authors	**111**

Note for Readers Outside the U.S.

Administrator, Principal and Vice Principal

The term "administrator" refers to principals and vice principals (or assistant principals). The principal and vice principal are analogous to the head teacher and deputy head in the British system. Elementary schools generally have only a principal, while middle schools and high schools may have a principal and one or more vice principals or assistant principals (depending on the size of the school).

"Administrator" also refers to more senior-level positions responsible for the oversight of multiple schools in a school district — an administrative unit comprised of schools within a geographic area.

Disciplinarian

The term "disciplinarian" is sometimes a job title. Typically, however, responsibility for carrying out disciplinary measures in a school falls to a designated vice principal, or the principal where there is no vice principal.

Types of Schools, Grades and Ages

The following chart shows the types of schools and corresponding grades and ages. The split between elementary and middle school and between middle school and high school varies.

SCHOOL	GRADE	AGES
Elementary school (primary)	Kindergarten	5–6
	1	6–7
	2	7–8
	3	8–9
	4	9–10
	5	10–11
Middle school (secondary)	6	11–12
(sometimes "junior high school")	7	12–13
	8	13–14
High school (secondary)	9 (freshman)	14–15
(sometimes "senior high school")	10 (sophomore)	15–16
	11 (junior)	16–17
	12 (senior)	17–18

New Thinking, New Practice, New Result

Introduction
New Thinking, New Practice, New Result

In 1998 a public high school in southeastern Pennsylvania started an educational program called the Academy. The Academy was a "school within a school" that offered students who were not very motivated by the conventional school curriculum the opportunity to participate in a project-oriented, interdisciplinary academic experience. The Academy collaborated with local businesses and other local agencies on video, web and graphic-design projects that offered students a range of real-world experiences. The goal was to connect what students were learning in school with real work they might be interested in doing when they graduated. The Academy was launched with about a hundred tenth- through twelfth-grade students.

Unfortunately, the reality of the Academy did not live up to the initial expectations. By midyear all the teachers were frustrated because, they said, the students were not behaving, and they couldn't teach the way they had hoped. Many of the students, only accustomed to working in teacher-centered traditional classroom settings, did not have the self-discipline and motivation necessary to work in a more independent, project-oriented environment. Further, they disrupted the work of those students who were more focused and motivated. Teachers, also accustomed to the usual dynamics and authority of the teacher-centered classroom, felt helpless and didn't know what to do about it. Traditional discipline strategies failed to create the kind of cooperative environment everyone had anticipated.

At this juncture our organization, the IIRP (International Institute for Restorative Practices), started working with the Academy. The IIRP grew out of the successful work of its sister organizations, the Community Service Foundation and Buxmont Academy, which operate programs for delinquent and at-risk youth in Pennsylvania. CSF Buxmont had developed and modeled the very restorative practices that would eventually impact not only the Academy, but the entire high school and eventually many other schools throughout the region and the world. The IIRP has since become a graduate school, but in those early days we only offered training and consulting. Although we now have a wealth of experience in working with other schools, our training and consulting division has its roots in the effective strategies CSF Buxmont programs use for working with the most challenging young people in eastern Pennsylvania. Many of them are adjudicated delinquent by juvenile court. Others are adjudicated dependent because of their ungovernable behavior at home. Many abuse drugs and alcohol or have mental health issues and come to us from residential mental health or drug rehabilitation facilities. Many others are sent to CSF Buxmont from public schools because of their unacceptable behavior.

In our eight schools and 16 group homes, we have created healthy, supportive environments that help young people grow and make positive changes in their lives. The IIRP began working with public schools in the late '90s. We felt that if we were able to achieve good results with the so-called "worst kids" in our region, we were confident that public schools could adapt our strategies to address behavior problems and build community in their classrooms. The goal was to create "Safer Saner Schools," which became the name of our training and consulting programs for educators.

Our initial efforts to train educators in public schools coincided with the urgent needs of the newly founded Academy, which was experiencing a crisis — the time when help is most desperately sought and most readily accepted. In response to their crisis, we offered to help them implement restorative practices.

The teachers were upset. They said, "All the students are misbehaving and acting out. We have no control." As consultants we said, "Let's take a closer look at the situation. It's probably not all the students. Let's

start by identifying which students are most responsible for your problems." As we developed the list, we urged them to think about which
students, if they were not in attendance on a particular day, would allow
for a good day at school. Ultimately they realized that it was fewer than
ten students who were consistently troublesome, but they influenced
and impacted others. "Great," we said. "Let's begin with them."

Shortly thereafter the vice principal of the school began calling
these "top ten" students to his office one at a time and said to each
of them: "Your behavior is affecting a lot of people in this program. I
know you're a leader. You have a lot of great qualities. But I see that the
way you're using these qualities is hurtful to a lot of people. How do
you think you're affecting people?"

He didn't scold the students. Rather, he started out by highlight-
ing leadership as a positive quality. But he did ask them to take a look
at their actions and how those actions were affecting others. Because
he made a distinction between how he felt about their behavior and
how he felt about them as people (what we call "separating the deed
from the doer"), the students felt comfortable responding.

The students were surprised that the vice principal wasn't simply
saying that they were bad or berating them. Instead, he acknowledged
their strengths while saying he didn't like some of their behavior, and
he gave them a chance to talk. The initial anger and fear the young
people brought with them into the office faded. The students began to
talk about their behavior, and some of them even admitted that they
knew how disruptive they could be.

Then the vice principal said, "Look, do you want to be in the
Academy? Your behavior says you don't. You can't keep behaving this
way. Do you want to be allowed to remain?"

All of them said, "Yes, we want to stay." After the students indi-
cated their choice, the vice principal asked them to make some verbal
commitments about how they were going to behave so that they could
continue in the Academy.

It may surprise the reader that these so-called "bad kids" chose
to stay in the program and agreed to cooperate, but we have found

more times than not that young people really do want to behave and participate when confronted with a clear choice and, simultaneously, with an opportunity to turn things around. We have found that troublesome students often find themselves stuck in a pattern of behavior that they don't know how to change. Our job is to teach them and to help them change.

Of course, one meeting didn't solve everything. But you have to start somewhere, and this intervention provided a real starting point for the Academy. When future problems arose the principal could say, "Remember your promises." Teachers, too, could refer to the commitments the students had made. At times throughout the year when problems arose, circles — which will be discussed extensively in this book — were convened in classrooms. These allowed other students to say for themselves how they were affected by the actions of disruptive students and to offer alternatives. The circles became a regular part of all classes, not only to deal with behavior problems, but as a everyday tool to enhance communication and build a sense of community. More significantly, teachers, disciplinarians and administrators in the school learned new ways to think about their roles and new ways to interact with students.

The adults showed respect toward students, both by holding them to a higher standard of behavior and by giving them the support they needed to become more responsible. We describe this dual approach as using both "high control" and "high support." By actively engaging students in this process, adults are doing things WITH students, rather than TO them or FOR them. By the end of the school year, the Academy was much closer to achieving its original expectations. Students, teachers, administrators and parents were happier, and the Academy continues to this day as an effective "school within a school" program.

The story of the Academy introduces a number of concepts that we refer to collectively as "restorative practices." The implementation of these practices in your classroom and your school will be the subject of this handbook.

The term "restorative practices" was derived from a significant development in the criminal justice field called "restorative justice." Our organization's awareness and subsequent involvement with restorative justice coincided with our own efforts to articulate and explain the methodology used in our CSF Buxmont programs to new staff and to others. Rather than simply punishing offenders, restorative justice holds offenders accountable for their crimes by involving them in face-to-face encounters with the people they have harmed. Research in restorative justice has revealed very positive outcomes for victims and offenders alike, including reduction in reoffending. Similar restorative practices in schools have yielded significant improvements in behavior and school climate as well.

Chapter One deals with the range of specific techniques that make up the spectrum of restorative practices. This chapter will give you ideas as to how you can begin to be restorative in response to a wide range of situations that may arise. Chapter Two focuses on the idea of discipline and looks at some concepts that help explain why and how restorative practices work. Chapter Three discusses how to implement changes and create a restorative atmosphere throughout a whole school.

While this book will discuss some of the theory of restorative justice and restorative practices, as a practical handbook this guide aims to be a useful reference and not a theoretical text. However, we do encourage you to learn more by exploring the resources cited at the end of this book.

Simply put, to be "restorative" means to believe that decisions are best made and conflicts are best resolved by those most directly involved in them. The restorative practices movement seeks to develop good relationships and restore a sense of community in an increasingly disconnected world. These practices have been applied in justice systems, families, workplaces and neighborhoods, as well as in schools.

There is a widely held mistaken belief that the concept of restorative practices is merely a discipline approach. While teachers have found these concepts and practices helpful in managing their class-rooms, the whole notion of actively engaging students and allowing them to take greater responsibility enhances the quality of teaching and learning in general. Such participatory strategies also have prac-tical implications for educating young people to take responsibility outside of school.

With the push for academic achievement and accountability, there seem to be many new mandates imposed on classroom teachers and school administrators, leaving less time for building relationships and connections with students. Paradoxically, without those relation-ships students feel less connected to school and are less likely to excel. This guide to using restorative practices in classrooms, in dealing with discipline, and in implementing change in your school will help you and your students improve relationships, behavior and decorum, all of which positively impact academic performance.

Ultimately, being restorative will require you to be creative in your responses to situations that arise in your classroom and your building. The following pages assist you by providing ideas and prac-tical strategies that you can use immediately.

Restorative Practices in the Classroom

Chapter 1
Restorative Practices in the Classroom

A few years ago we met a high school English teacher who was really struggling with one of her ninth-grade classes. Every day the students were disrespectful and disruptive. They criticized and made fun of all her assignments and activities. She tried to be more creative and tailor the class to be more fun and interesting for them, but no matter what she did, nothing seemed to work. She felt like there was nothing she could do to change things.

After she talked to an IIRP consultant, she formulated a new plan of action. She pulled two ringleaders aside after class, told them that she was frustrated with their behavior and said the following: "While you guys might not like English class, I work very hard to make this class interesting. I don't think it is fair for you to say that assignments are 'stupid' without even giving them a chance, and it hurts my feelings. I'd like you to make a commitment to not do that anymore." They seemed surprised at her directness but agreed to her request.

Several weeks later she reported that the class had gotten better, but that she wasn't absolutely sure that her discussion with the two students had anything to do with it. Perhaps it was a coincidence.

Then, a month later, the teacher found herself with a new student in her class who transferred from another school district. While she was handing out a worksheet, the new student muttered loud enough for her to hear, "Man, this is so stupid!" Both of the students she had previously talked with came to her defense. They immediately spoke up and told him: "Don't say that. She really works hard on this stuff!"

INFORMAL				FORMAL
affective statements	affective questions	small impromptu conference	group or circle	formal conference

Figure 1. Restorative Practices Continuum.

Affective Statements

The way the classroom teacher talked to her students is similar to the way the principal talked to the students in the story in the Introduction. In this instance you have a teacher, rather than an administrator, confronting the students. Teachers sometimes think they don't have a lot of power to influence their students, but here we see in a very informal exchange that the teacher's feelings alone counted for a lot. All that the teacher really did, without embarrassing the students, was to give the students a little information about herself. She told them she works hard to make the class interesting, and she asked them to promise to give her assignments a chance.

The teacher used what we call "affective statements" (see p. 68 for more on the psychology of affect). That is, she told the students how they affected her. Affective statements are the most informal type of response on the "Restorative Practices Continuum" (see Figure 1). This chapter will discuss the whole range of restorative responses, from informal to formal. Along with affective questions, affective statements are some of the easiest and most useful tools for building a restorative classroom. When a teacher sets a more positive tone on a day-to-day basis, more serious problems that require more serious responses tend to diminish in both intensity and frequency.

The term "affective statements" is just another way of saying "expressing your feelings," and it's a crucial first step. Understanding and using such statements can help foster an immediate change in the dynamic between teacher and student. When you tell a student how you feel, you are humanizing yourself to students, who often perceive teachers as distinct from themselves. Some teachers have expressed a concern that sharing their feelings will make them appear weak to their students or that students will take advantage of them for being vulnerable. We have found just the opposite to be true. When you express your feelings, children become more, not less, empathetic. Affective statements help you build a relationship based on students' new image of you as someone who cares and has feelings, rather than as a distant authority figure.

We should strive to express both pleasant and unpleasant feelings. We have repeatedly found that many students are completely unaware of the impact — positive and negative — that their behavior has on others. Students will learn that you genuinely care about them and are truly excited when they do well. They will also learn that when they fail to meet expectations, it was more than just a norm or rule that was violated. Their relationship with you and others was also violated.

Affective statements can be used to acknowledge success, hard work, collaboration or any other desirable behavior. The more specific you are about what the student did and how you feel, the better. "Good job today, Sam" is much less meaningful than "Sam, I was really happy that you worked for the entire class period today." When you take the time to verbally express your feelings by saying, for example, "It was a joy for me to see the way you developed that project," you are going beyond the good grade written on the paper. You are giving the feedback a personal dimension. If you are out sick one day and the next day a student asks if you are feeling better, instead of just saying, "I feel better" or "Thanks for asking," you can say, "It means a lot to me that you would ask how I'm feeling." (See Figure 2 for more examples.)

Similarly, when a student's behavior causes concern, the more specific and emotive you can be, the better. "I'm upset" is better than "That is inappropriate." But a statement like "Lisa, I'm frustrated that you keep disrupting class today" is even more powerful. Similarly, "Don, I was shocked when I graded your paper. You are capable of doing much better" not only expresses your surprise at poor academic performance but also helps to separate the deed from the doer by sharing that you care about the student.

Frequently students will be more receptive to affective statements if they are delivered privately. Sometimes this is not practical and sometimes a public comment is more appropriate. Statements made publicly in an attempt to embarrass a student, however, almost always backfire. No teacher would enjoy being confronted publicly by the school principal for something the teacher was doing wrong. Young people are sensitive, too, and we have to show them respect, encourage them to express their feelings and try not to hurt them.

If you confront a child in front of the entire class when a private intervention is just as feasible, we might not define that as a restorative response, even if you are expressing your feelings. That goes for almost everything we talk about in this book. If you treat a student in a demeaning manner, it undermines the potential for improving your relationship with the student. "Restorative" means changing your own attitude, and it also means believing in students even when — and especially when — they seem to be behaving badly.

A student went into a rage one morning when she received a paper back from a teacher. There were corrections marked all over it and the grade was very low. The student stood up and started cursing at the teacher and couldn't be mollified. She left the class and stomped through the halls of the school shouting about how angry she was and how terrible the teacher was. The principal heard her and by this time had gotten the story from the teacher. The girl had been to the principal's office before and they had a relationship. The principal approached the angry student and calmly said, "I'm so proud of you. I never knew you cared this much about your schoolwork and what your teacher thought of you."

This literally stopped the student in her tracks and she began to cry. In this moment, by reframing the student's anger, a positive resolution to the problem came to light. The student was ashamed to receive a bad mark and she was lashing out. The affective statement — "I am so proud of you" — sincerely given, surprised the student. It was the last thing she expected to hear. The next statement, which provided the reason the principal felt proud, affirmed the student's desire to do well in school. In the same instant it gave the student a chance to see how her own behavior was out of line. Eventually, the student could discuss different and more appropriate responses to getting a bad grade. She went back and apologized to the teacher and found out what she could do to improve her grade.

TYPICAL RESPONSE	AFFECTIVE STATEMENT
» Stop teasing Sandy.	» It makes me uncomfortable when I hear you teasing Sandy.
» Talking during class is inappropriate.	» I am frustrated that you aren't listening to me.
» You shouldn't do that.	» I feel sad when you say something like that to John.
» Sit down and be quiet.	» I get angry when you talk and joke during my lectures.
» I don't want to see you fighting with him.	» I was shocked to see you hurt Pete.

Figure 2. Other examples of affective statements.

Informal affective statements can be offered when you see a child doing something that makes you uncomfortable as a teacher. They offer an alternative when you are tired of saying, "Don't do that," "Stop that" or "Don't you think you're being inappropriate?"

During a coed softball game, a girl was being flirtatious with the boys. At one point she put the catcher's mitt over her crotch and laughed. Later, the teacher discreetly called the girl over to her and said: "When you did that earlier, it made me really sad for you. You are a beautiful girl, and you don't have to do things like that to get boys to like you." The girl looked at the teacher and smiled and said, "Thank you."

Some teachers feel uncomfortable confronting issues and prefer to ignore and avoid the situation. But small affective exchanges, over a period of time, can have a huge positive impact on students.

Affective Questions

Accepting that conflict is an integral part of life is crucial to adopting restorative practices. There will always be misunderstandings, competing needs and interests, and differences of opinion. In a school the students will not always behave as you wish. Dealing with conflict is part of an educator's job, whether we like it or not. Restorative practices helps to revise our thinking so that we see conflict in a school setting as an opportunity to foster learning and build better relationships.

WHEN CHALLENGING BEHAVIOR	TO HELP THOSE AFFECTED
» What happened?	» What did you think when you realized what had happened?
» What were you thinking of at the time?	
» What have you thought about since?	» What impact has this incident had on you and others?
» Who has been affected by what you have done? In what way have they been affected?	» What has been the hardest thing for you?
» What do you think you need to do to make things right?	» What do you think needs to happen to make things right?

Figure 3. Restorative questions.

We make a distinction between punishment and natural or restorative kinds of consequences. In the case of the girl who exploded when she got a bad grade, punishment would have only reinforced her sense of outrage. She was upset. Her tears showed she was feeling remorse. Instead of punishment, the natural consequence of her actions was that she needed to do something to restore her place in the classroom. She cared about that class and that teacher, although at first glance we might not have suspected it. The natural consequence of her inappropriate behavior was to apologize to the teacher and ask what she could do to return to the class and earn a better grade.

She also had to ask the teacher how she felt about what had happened and what the teacher thought needed to happen in order to make things right. These are two of the affective questions, which, along with affective statements, are crucial tools. We also call these questions "restorative questions" (see Figure 3).

In 1995 Terry O'Connell, a former Australian police officer and restorative justice pioneer (now director of Real Justice Australia, an IIRP affiliate), provided training in "restorative conferencing" for our CSF Buxmont staff. (Restorative conferencing is further explained later in this chapter.) He emphasized the power of the restorative questions and talked about how effective he had found them for working with offenders and victims of crime. We had been using similar questions for many years on a daily basis in our counseling programs, schools and group homes, but we had never formulated a list like the one above. Susan Wachtel, the co-founder of CSF Buxmont, was working in one of our schools the day after the training, and she decided to put these restorative questions to the test.

Susan observed a student behaving inappropriately toward a teacher in a class. She asked the teacher if she could talk to the student privately. When she and the student were seated in another room, she simply asked, "What happened?" and got quiet. The boy, who initially was angry about being removed from the class, surprised Susan with his willingness to respond to the question. He candidly told Susan what he had been doing to bother the teacher.

Since the first question worked, she continued, working her way through the list of questions. "I sat there amazed at what the kid was saying," Susan reports in retelling the story of her experiment. "When I asked him how his behavior had affected the teacher, he said,

'The teacher probably felt embarrassed. I think he was really mad. I know I got him off track.' The boy was so sincere, I was shocked."

Susan went on to the next question: "Who else do you think was affected?" He said, "The kids in the class."

Then she asked, "How do you think they were affected?" He said: "I know some kids were mad because they couldn't concentrate. I know some kids were interested and they were distracted. My friend told me to be quiet, but I didn't listen to him."

Susan continued, "Well, how were you affected?" He said: "I'm disappointed in myself. I need to get a good grade, and I hurt my chances for that."

By now the kid was clearly remorseful, no longer angry. Susan said, "How would you like to repair the harm that was done?" He answered: "Oh, I really want to apologize to my teacher. And then I think I want to apologize to my class."

"When are you going to do that?" asked Susan. He responded, "When class is over I'll talk to the teacher."

And the boy did just what he said. The teacher was also surprised and couldn't believe how sincere the student was. The exchange took about ten minutes. And everyone — teacher, student and class — benefited.

This story illustrates how useful the entire list of questions can be, but you will more often use just one or two of these questions in an informal way for a quick exchange lasting a couple of minutes. Nonetheless, each intervention, no matter how brief, provides an important opportunity for young people to reflect on the impact of their behavior and to learn empathy for those whom they have affected.

If two students are arguing in the lunchroom, for example, you might call them over one at a time and ask them individually, "What happened?" Depending on what they say, you could add, "How do you feel when Karen does that?" or "How do you think she feels when you do that?" Then you might bring the students together and ask them the same questions so they can hear how they've affected each other. Finally, you can ask each of them what they can do to make things right. (When you bring the students together like this, you are actually conducting a "small impromptu conference," which we'll cover more in the next section.)

Getting students to speak and find solutions is a significant shift for teachers and administrators. Usually we, as educators, find ourselves constantly correcting students' behavior, which gets rather tiresome. We have come to believe that telling children what not to do is a necessary part of our job and we don't see any options or alternatives. The affective questions can be helpful here because they let you turn the tables. You still address inappropriate behavior but in a way that asks students to think for themselves about their actions and to reflect on how they affect other people. That shifts responsibility away from you and places it on the students whose behavior is causing the problem.

In the previous section we described how affective statements allow you to express your feelings to a student. Affective questions help to elicit what a student is thinking and feeling and therefore many of their responses will be affective statements. Of course there are other questions that can be asked to help students better understand the impact of behavior, both theirs and others'. The ones listed in Figure 3 are a distillation of the questions we have found to be most helpful.

Notice that "Why did you do that?" is absent from the list. That question is really not helpful or relevant. Young people usually don't know why they did something wrong. In all likelihood they were simply being thoughtless or impetuous, without any reason. And if they have to dig for a reason it often ends up being a rationalization or justification. What is more effective is to foster a process of reflection by asking questions that will get the misbehaving young people to think about their behavior and how it impacted others.

The second column of questions in Figure 3 can be asked of those who have been affected by the inappropriate behavior. For example, if a student cheated by glancing at another student's work, the second student could be asked, "What did you think when you realized what had happened?" A lot of times the teacher simply punishes the offending student. While the teacher may still have to decide on the consequence for cheating, merely punishing a student forgoes a critical learning opportunity. In fact, it's not the teacher who has been harmed by the cheating as much as the other students in the class. They're working hard and here is an individual trying to take advantage of their efforts.

Of course, you have to use your own judgment to decide whether to deal with the problem privately or in front of other students. It may depend on the age and the personalities of the students themselves. We'll deal with those considerations more in Chapter Two.

Another important technique is to have the restorative questions listed on a piece of paper that can be handed to a student. Although it would be great if we always had enough time to sit down and talk things through with every student, that isn't always possible. Instead, asking a student to write down responses to the restorative questions on a sheet of paper may be more practical. Further, it promotes reflection and allows tempers to cool, including yours. It also allows you to give immediate attention to the problem without interrupting what you've been doing with the other students in the class. Also, you might consider this time spent by the student in reflecting and writing as a way of providing a "time out" for older students.

Of course, asking restorative questions is only restorative if you use them properly. Bob, one of the authors of this book, remembers a time when he decided to use the questions with his 8-year-old daughter shortly after he learned about them. She misbehaved and Bob, at the top of his lungs, yelled, "What were you thinking?!" which did not promote the useful reflection associated with restorative practices. It is not that you must always be calm and never be angry. Showing emotions is natural, but restorative strategies don't work if your tone is purely punitive. When used appropriately, however, restorative practices can move the situation from anger to a more productive resolution.

A teacher at a suburban school just outside a major city says he uses a restorative approach in everyday interactions with students. "When I see a kid acting up in the hallway, instead of immediately dragging him into the discipline office, I'll pull him over, one-on-one, and try to find out exactly what's happening and understand where he's coming from," he explained. "A lot of times it's not the specific incident that's caused the conflict, but rather something that's happened earlier in the day or at home or in a previous class. Allowing that venting process tends to diffuse it, along with the feeling that an adult is listening and caring."

Small Impromptu Conferences

A high school teacher saw a student push another student's books out of his hands, and it looked like the two were about to start to fight. She pulled them aside in the hallway and said, "Hey, what happened here?" and she let each student talk. She said to the one who lost his books, "How were you affected by that?" The student replied that it made him really angry. The teacher expressed her feelings, too, by saying: "I don't feel safe in the halls when students are fighting. I needed to get to another classroom, but I feel responsible when I see something like this." Lastly, she asked the students to say what they wanted to see happen to resolve the issue. They promised not to fight and they both apologized to one another and to the teacher. No one was late for class.

When something happens in a class, on a field trip, in the lunchroom or in the hallway and it affects multiple people, a small impromptu conference is an effective response. Building on the affective questions, this can bring everyone involved in the incident together and resolve the problem relatively quickly.

Small negative incidents like the one in the hallway accumulate and have an overall impact in your class and in your school. The purpose of a small impromptu conference is to address a problem to keep it from escalating and to resolve the problem quickly, but in a way that gets students actively engaged in expressing their feelings and in thinking about the impact of their behavior and about how to resolve conflicts.

For example, two girls on the playground are fighting to go down the slide first. A teacher might yell at them and say: "You're going to hurt each other. You need to stop arguing and cooperate. Why don't you take turns? Sally, you go first and then you, Andrea." That may stop the problem for the moment, but the kids may still be angry and feel unresolved.

Instead, an impromptu conference might go like this: "Sally, Andrea, would you please come over here? I was really scared for you when I saw you fighting on the slide. What happened?" After each girl talks, say to each in turn, "What was your part in what happened?" One might try to blame the other, but you can say: "We're talking about just you right now. What was your part in this?" Finally, you can ask them, "Now what can you each do to make this better?"

People like to have their say. By asking the questions, you let each child reflect on how she added to the conflict, and then each can say how she wants the situation to be resolved. The teacher becomes a facilitator, rather than just a disciplinarian.

The last question about how to make things better is critical because it is reintegrative in nature. Punishments can leave kids feeling ashamed and embarrassed. By separating the deed from the doer, we are telling young people that we respect them, but that we don't like a particular behavior they have been doing. When they say what they can do to make it better, they can then move on with their day without the unresolved feeling of "I'm a bad person."

In some cases, you can go a step further by creating an opportunity to follow up with the students. You might ask, "What is one thing each of you will do differently now to make sure this doesn't happen again?" and allow each student to respond. Then end by asking, "Which one of you can come by my classroom at the end of school today to let me know how it went?" or "Tomorrow, I want you both to let me know how the rest of the day was." Commitments give students something specific and constructive to try and achieve.

The follow-up helps reintegrate the students, so they know they are no longer in trouble and that they can consider themselves in good standing as far as you are concerned.

Circles

As a symbol of community, circles are one of the most distinctive and flexible forms of restorative practices. Just sitting in a circle creates the feeling that a group of people is connected, and when the teacher sits among the students, it enhances the quality of their relationships. While circles can be used as a response to wrongdoing, they are also very effective as a proactive process for building social capital and creating classroom norms. Teachers can use circles to check in with students at the beginning of the day or before certain classes to help students with planning, to set ground rules for projects and activities, and to deal with more serious problems in a class.

A fifth-grade class began holding circle meetings every morning. At first the students were resistant, but soon they became accustomed to the circles and to talking with their peers each day. As the school year came to an end, a visitor happened to be in the class during a morning meeting and was invited to sit within the circle. The visitor asked the children if anything had changed since they had started using circles every day. The teacher felt a little uncomfortable, unsure if the students were aware of the improvements. Much to the teacher's surprise, the students, each in turn, spoke eloquently about how they had become more respectful of each other because they had learned more about each other and how they now recognized their common membership in the classroom community.

Two significant developments were made apparent by the visitor's question. While the teacher may have been aware of improvements in the classroom, she now realized that her fifth-grade students understood the benefits of the circle meetings as well. Secondly, the students demonstrated that they felt comfortable making observations about themselves, even in front of a guest.

The most common way to do a circle meeting is to arrange students' chairs in a circle, ask a question and have students respond in turn going around the circle. This "go-around" technique is the simplest and easiest to manage. It helps to use a "talking piece," a symbolic object that can be passed around from student to student, designating the only person who has the right to speak. Although you don't have to use a talking piece, it is important that no one interrupt the speaker. Students must patiently wait until their turn to speak. This circle go-around method creates remarkable decorum.

Only the teacher may interact with the speaker or ask a clarifying question in the circle go-around, but even this should be done with discrimination. Everyone needs to feel that she has the opportunity to say what she needs to say. One of the most important benefits of this go-around strategy is that it affords quieter students opportunities to be heard without having to compete with more assertive students. Interestingly, these quiet students often make the most valuable contributions to the discussion.

"Check-in." At the beginning of class, you may do a go-around in which each student responds to a question or statement like:

- How are you feeling today?
- What is one of your academic goals for the day?
- Make a commitment about your behavior in school today.
- Review something you accomplished last week.

Praise students for their participation, even if they struggle to come up with something or seem reluctant to speak. Assume that students' apparent resistance, whether they act silly, interrupt other students while they are talking or refuse to talk at all, is motivated by anxiety and not disrespect for you. Their discomfort will dissipate quickly if you are confident and positive about the activity and address their behavior in a firm but caring way. For example, you might say, "Sam, you seem to think this is funny, but I would really appreciate it if you would take this circle seriously."

Also, it is helpful if the teacher and other adults present participate and model the kinds of responses and behavior they would like to see from the students. For example, you may choose to be the first to answer the question. This will help put students at ease, give them a chance to know you better and set the tone for the go-around.

"**Check-out.**" At the end of a day or a class, do a go-around in which each student responds to a question or statement like:
- How was your day today?
- Say one thing you liked about this class today.
- What is one thing you learned today?
- What are you looking forward to for school tomorrow?

Classroom norms. Classroom norms deal with the expectations and procedures for a particular class. Engaging students in a discussion about how students should act and how they can all work to enforce those expectations changes the nature of classroom management. It is advantageous to carry out this sort of discussion in a circle. Instead of the traditional arrangement of a teacher unilaterally making and enforcing behavior expectations, classroom management becomes a collaborative process with shared responsibility and ownership. Here are some questions you might ask to begin a discussion about norms:
- What helps you to learn while you are in class?
- What stops you from learning?
- In order for us to have a successful year together, what are some things we can agree on related to how we will all behave and treat each other?
- How should we respond if someone fails to keep these agreements?

The more engaging you make this process, the more ownership students will take. Starting with "Here are the rules of my classroom. How are you going to follow them?" will not have significant impact. Asking the students to suggest the rules and expectations is preferable. You might have them write up the norms on a large piece of paper and post them in the class for later reference. Interestingly, you will find that students identify and share most of the expectations that you have. When students suggest these norms themselves, they will be more likely to take responsibility for them. In our CSF Buxmont programs, populated by some of the most challenging youth in our region, we have found that engaging students in this process dramatically improves compliance with behavioral norms.

Classroom content. An economics and entrepreneurship teacher in a high school was concerned that the students in one of his classes were not staying on task and that several students were repeatedly distracting the others. The teacher decided to run a circle for the whole class to focus the class on the academic content, but not on the challenging behavior. Instead he made the circle discussion topic what he had been trying to accomplish in class. As they went around the circle, students were asked to "talk about your own strengths and weaknesses in terms of owning and operating a small business." The teacher and his assistant went first to model what they expected. All of the students, including those who had been causing most of the problems, participated appropriately. The teacher later observed, "It was amazing that by using this process, integrating curriculum content with restorative practices, the class went so well." He added, "Since that time, I have integrated curriculum to reinforce to all students that their ideas and feelings do matter and have an effect on the class in general."

The teacher found that circles were a useful tool for carrying out academic business. In order to make children feel comfortable speaking in circles and using circles, you must use circles in a variety of ways. In doing so, you will find that the use of circles can directly serve the academic purposes of your class by engaging students more actively in their own learning.

Academic goals. The circle can also become a tool for academic goal setting. Students can use circles to establish plans for the coming class period, the coming week or the upcoming unit of study. This type of circle transforms your students' educational experience from that of passive recipient to active participant and planner. In addition to learning the course content, circles weave the critical skills of goal setting and monitoring into the daily classroom experience. Examples of questions you might use include:

- What is your goal for class this week?
- What is something you need in order to get your work done today?
- What steps will you complete this week toward carrying out your project?

Besides goal setting, circles can be a useful tool for monitoring progress. By creating a feedback loop, students can comment on their own accomplishments. Instead of being accountable only to the teacher, students will want to show their peers that they are being successful in school. Students can also give constructive feedback to one another:

- What accomplishments have you made in this class in the past month?
- Who is someone in this class who worked hard this week?
- What is the most useful thing you've learned this year?
- Who is someone who helped you?
- What is something you know how to do that you didn't know how to do last year?
- Say something positive about a member of the class.

Circles can merge the goals of community building and academic achievement so that students are strengthening relationships while addressing content areas.

Behavior problems. At first, when circles are new to you and your students, they may feel awkward. Students may seem shy and resistant. But once circles have been established as a normal part of the classroom routine, at the beginning of each class, at the beginning and ending of the week, or perhaps every Wednesday, students will become very comfortable with the process. Teachers find that once they've established a routine of conducting circles, students will express concern if a circle doesn't happen at the appointed time.

As comfort, trust and expectations increase, circles present themselves as an excellent tool for responding to significant behavior problems that arise in the classroom. When only one or two students misbehave, it may be more appropriate to deal with the situations individually or in a small impromptu conference as described above. However, when misbehavior either involves or affects a larger group of students, or when the teacher wants to address a pattern of behavior rather than a specific instance, circles make it possible to respond to the problem, air feelings, repair the harm, address issues and plan changes for the future.

There are many circumstances in which a teacher can't even pinpoint exactly why he has a bad feeling. Our inclination might be to ignore those subtle twinges of discomfort or to hope the problem will eventually fade away. In contrast, in our CSF Buxmont schools and group homes, we always tell our staff, "If it doesn't feel right, it's not right." It never hurts to bring up an issue in a restorative way. In almost every instance that a teacher feels something isn't quite right, students are feeling just as uneasy. Additionally, engaging young people in talking with their peers about behavior is a wonderful educational opportunity.

A ninth-grade teacher ran a circle to address an underlying feeling of friction that she was sensing among the students in her classroom. She decided to use a circle after she heard a girl express that other students were getting in the way of her learning. Based on the comments from the other students in the circle, however, the girl came to the realization that she was actually causing most of the problem herself. "That was a really hard day and students were in tears," said the teacher. "But after the circle the entire class got along fine." The teacher said that she often uses circles for dealing with behavior problems: "I can just say: 'This is how I'm feeling. How are you feeling? And what are we going to do to work together?'"

During these circles for addressing behavior problems, the restorative questions listed earlier can be used, but a variety of other questions may be helpful.

- What was your part in the problem?
- What can we do to make sure this doesn't happen again?
- How do you feel when you get teased? (or when students make jokes while the teacher is talking, or whatever the inappropriate behavior may be)

When the circle does involve one or two identified "offenders," be sure to praise them publicly for their courage in dealing with the incident in such a public way. Always look for ways to reintegrate them and allow them to reclaim their good names in the class.

A teacher had a stress ball shaped like an apple (a ball that you can squeeze in your hand to relieve stress) that she kept on her desk. She allowed students to use it, but one day the teacher noticed that the stem was missing from the apple. She was angry. She circled up her students and told them that she wanted to know who did it and that she wanted the stress ball to be replaced. In going around the circle, students identified one boy who then admitted what he had done: "I liked the ball. I was playing with it and the stem broke. I felt really bad, but I didn't know what to do, so I just put it back on the desk without saying anything." He was very sincere, acknowledging that he had handled the situation badly and offering to buy another one for the teacher. But as a result of his sincere apology the teacher was feeling better and said: "No, I don't need you to buy another one. That's what I thought I wanted at first. But now I can see that all I wanted was for the problem to be acknowledged. Thanks for getting honest."

Circles can be used to address behavior problems when you don't know who did something, like the example above, even when it is unlikely that anyone will accept responsibility. For example, if there are occasional incidents of petty theft, it is unlikely that a circle will identify the culprits. But you might initiate a circle go-around to help address the issue by asking each student to answer the two questions "Have you ever had something stolen from you?" and "What was it and how did it make you feel when that happened?" Or you can identify the problem by saying: "Things are getting stolen around our classroom. It would be great to know who is doing it, but let's just talk about theft and how you felt in the past when something was stolen from you."

The circle brings to consciousness the whole issue of stealing in a general way. Those who are taking things will hear from others how that makes other people feel and causes them to reflect on their own behavior. In fact, they themselves will also have to talk about how they felt when something was taken from them. It is possible that the individuals who are responsible for the thefts will speak up and admit their wrongdoing. In our CSF Buxmont programs, that happens occasionally. More often we have found that, even if the guilty parties don't admit their wrongdoing, the stealing stops.

In one of our CSF Buxmont schools someone stole money from a teacher's purse. In the circle the teacher told all the students that she didn't have a lot of money and that she was planning on using it to pay for cable television. She talked about how excited her own children were about this, but that now she would have to explain to them that she couldn't pay for it because the money was stolen. The students in the circle emotionally expressed their sympathy for the teacher and her children, and even though the culprit was never found, the teacher reported that she felt better just hearing what the students had to say. When you have had something stolen, your whole perspective can change and you may feel mistrustful of everyone. But in this case, the circle provided an opportunity for students to show their support to the teacher and help make her more comfortable in the school community.

In another similar situation at CSF Buxmont, students decided to each contribute a dollar or two to pay back a sum of money that was stolen. In yet another instance of theft, the students volunteered to hold a bake sale to raise the money to pay someone back. Although we always want to know "whodunit," we will rarely achieve that goal. But the use of circles can help the classroom or school community achieve other important goals that we usually overlook, like acknowledging the feelings of victims and offering them communal support. Using circle go-arounds, we can highlight the consequences of stealing, acknowledge the victim's feelings and restore a sense of well-being to the community.

Issues like teasing or bullying or cheating can also be addressed indirectly, without confronting the offender. You might start a go-around in a circle by saying, "Name a time you got bullied and talk about what that was like." Alternatively, you could also say, "Name a time you bullied someone and describe what that was like." So without pointing fingers, especially when the problem is general or you don't have "proof" or the victim is too embarrassed to step forward, you can still confront the issue, explore the feelings and highlight the impact on others that is associated with the behavior.

Being proactive. While restorative techniques are a good way to respond to wrongdoing, they are equally important as proactive measures to avoid potential problems.

At a vocational school that was just beginning its use of restorative practices, a culinary arts teacher decided to try running a circle for his students at the beginning of the school year. The kitchen was a notoriously tough classroom. Even though there were only 15 students, they worked in close physical proximity, stress levels ran high and there were always conflicts. The dropout rate for the multiyear program was also high, with students quitting the program during or after the first year.

What was intended as a brief circle to introduce new students and begin the new school year turned into a lengthy discussion. The students took over the direction of the circle and the teacher decided to follow their lead. Returning students told their stories and talked about their fears and frustrations. The circle went on for three hours.

Several days later the teacher invited the vocational school principal into the class and asked the kids to talk about the circle on the first day. Students said: "I found out my problems aren't that bad. When we're in the kitchen and things are happening, we now understand why people are stressed out or doing certain things. It's better now when we work in the kitchen because we're like a team or a family." During that school year not a single student quit the culinary program.

Another very useful application of proactive circles is in preparation for taking students on a field trip. Hold a circle and ask the students to answer some questions about the upcoming trip such as:

- How might you be tempted to act out on this trip?
- What kind of impression do you want to make on people where we're going?
- What do you think is the appropriate way to act in an art museum?
- List some "dos and don'ts" for this trip.
- How will you deal with any disagreements or problems you face with other students if something does happen?

You can use these kinds of proactive questions in a circle format any time you are attempting a new type of activity or are going to do something with students where you know there is a potential for inappropriate behavior, such as watching a feature-length movie or playing a game in class. At our CSF Buxmont programs, where we bring together some of the most impulsive young people in our region, we have found that getting them to anticipate potential problems is a remarkably effective way to reduce the likelihood that those problems will ever occur. Raising consciousness reduces impulsivity.

Some tips for running circles. As teachers, you want circles to be a tool for building relationships and solving problems, but, of course, you are not counselors or social workers and you don't want circles to take over all the time in your class. Many of the simple go-around exercises and check-ins or check-outs can be done in a few minutes. Some tips to help you have your circles go smoothly are:

- Set clear topics and goals for the outcome of the circle.
- Set a positive tone. If you are confident and upbeat, the students will follow your lead.
- Keep the focus. In a kind and supportive way, make sure the conversation sticks to the goal you have set.
- Make students your allies. For example, you can tell several students before an upcoming circle, "I'm counting on you to speak up today," and ask them to speak first.
- Always sit in the circle with students and participate fully.

The more circles you run, the easier they'll get. While we have provided many examples here, ultimately, you're going to have to be responsive to situations as they arise. This book is just a guide. If you want a new idea for a go-around question, make one up. You can always run a circle where you say, "Talk about a pet you have, you had or you want" or "What do you hope to do this weekend?" The more students get to know each other and get to know you, the stronger will be the bonds that connect you. From a classroom management perspective, when people feel connected to one another through mutual understanding and empathy, they are less likely to misbehave or treat each other disrespectfully.

Formal Conferences

There are basically two types of formal conferences, although there are many variations and names given to these. The first is "restorative conferencing" and the second is "family group decision making" (FGDM) or "family group conferencing" (FGC).

Restorative conferences. Restorative conferences are formal responses to wrongdoing where all those involved and affected by an incident come together with a trained facilitator to explore what happened, who was affected and what needs to be done to make things right. The participants include those who did the wrong and those who were affected by the wrong, often including the family or friends of both parties. A fight, incident of drug possession or other serious infraction in school (which may involve a police response) might be appropriate for such a process. The conference takes a fair amount of time to organize and carry out and is facilitated by someone who has not been directly involved. A formal conference is not a routine classroom process run by the teacher, like circles, but is typically organized by someone else, often under the jurisdiction of the school administration.

The restorative conference model taught by the IIRP is called a "Real Justice" conference. It involves a script that the facilitator follows to ask a series of open-ended questions of each and every participant in the conference. The responses, of course, are not scripted. The original purpose of the script, when developed by former Australian police officer Terry O'Connell, was to limit the facilitator's role in the conference. The facilitator is supposed to avoid interfering in the discussion and the decisions made by the participants in the conference. So O'Connell devised what he called the script and instructed the facilitator to confine his or her involvement to the written text that opens and closes the conference, the questions that are prescribed for offenders, victims and their supporters, and occasional but very limited interventions to keep the conference on track.

The following is the story of a restorative conference that was used to resolve a significant harassment problem on a school bus. Students from an alternative school for troubled youth and students from a private school traveled together on the school bus every morning and afternoon. A boy and a girl from the alternative school regularly teased and taunted two brothers from another school, making cruel jokes about the fact that they were Jewish. The mother of the boys who were being abused called the principal of the alternative school and told her what was happening. The principal was extremely embarrassed and apologetic. As a possible remedy for the situation, she asked the mother if she and her children would be willing to participate in a restorative conference. The mother agreed and the conference was arranged.

When the conference convened, 18 people were present. The group included the students directly involved in the incident, other students from the bus and from each school who were there to support them, parents, a couple of teachers and the principal who had suggested the conference.

The conference facilitator, in this case a teacher from another school, welcomed the participants and explained that the purpose of the conference was to explore what had happened, how people were affected and what could be done to repair the harm.

First, the facilitator asked the offenders to talk about what happened. At this point their parents inappropriately interfered in the process, wanting to defend their children from being characterized as bad or hurtful. Their children's school principal, who was familiar with the conference process, assured the parents that everyone would get a turn to express their feelings and that all of the participants wanted to resolve this issue with a positive outcome. The parents quieted down and let the facilitator proceed.

The offenders, prompted with the questions from the facilitator, took responsibility for their behavior. They talked about thoughts and feelings they had since the incident. They realized that they were wrong in what they did and wanted to apologize. They talked about how they thought the two brothers had been affected by what they had done.

The event became very emotional. The brothers talked about how they were afraid on the bus and that they were ashamed and embarrassed to be treated this way. Eventually everyone got a chance to speak. Interestingly, the friends of both the offenders and their victims were upset by the harassment. One African-American girl from the alternative school, who was a friend of the offenders, expressed her dismay at what they had done. She said she understood how badly the Jewish boys felt because she knew how she felt when others made derogatory racial comments to her.

During the last part of the conference, everyone was asked what outcome they'd like from the conference and how amends could be made, and formal agreements were drawn up. Mostly what the brothers and their mother wanted was assurance that this would not happen again.

After most formal conferences, refreshments are served. People symbolically "break bread" together and enjoy the informal atmosphere that allows them to reintegrate with one another after the formality of the conference. In this case, the parents of all the children talked. The Jewish mother invited the students who had harassed her sons and their parents to her daughter's bat mitzvah. The principal noted that "it was a remarkable event."

Conferences like this one are the most formal choice on the Restorative Practices Continuum. As mentioned above, such events do not typically occur during a normal class period. A teacher may be asked to attend such a meeting as a participant, and interested teachers may be trained to facilitate restorative conferences. Understanding restorative conferences fosters insight into all other restorative practices. Educators find the Real Justice conferencing training especially useful because it includes realistic role plays that allow everyone to experience the different perspectives — victim, offender, parent, facilitator — thereby promoting empathy and illustrating the potential of restorative practices.

Family group decision making. Family group decision making (FGDM) or family group conferencing (FGC) are events where decisions and plans need to be made about a young person. These meetings are characterized by a high level of family involvement and often include extended family and friends. The crucial component of this type of conference is the "family alone time" when the professionals leave the room and the family members and the young person work out a plan together.

FGDM or FGC has three parts. First, the professionals, who might be social workers, probation officers, school counselors or police, outline the problems, the legal situation and the various resources available to serve the child and family. The second part is called "family alone time," where the professionals leave the room and the family and others in the child's community of care, such as neighbors or a pastor, discuss and develop a written plan. In the third part, the professionals are called back into the room, and the family explains the plan to them.

Depending on the setting, the professionals may immediately accept the plan. For instance, a school administrator or counselor may have the authority to make such a decision. In social services settings, a social worker may support the plan and recommend it to a juvenile court or family court judge. These family group conferences, originating in New Zealand in 1989, have a longer history in social welfare and juvenile justice than in schools. But they are increasingly used in educational settings to deal with ongoing behavioral difficulties, truancy, school phobia and bullying, either by or of the young person. They are sometimes used as an alternative to suspension or expulsion.

A 10-year-old boy was on the verge of expulsion from his elementary school. His inappropriate behavior was taking up hours of his teacher's time each week. The school organized a conference that included the boy's mother, his father, who no longer lived with the boy's mother, the father's new partner, siblings, aunts, uncles, a woman who worked in the lunchroom, and the postman who delivered mail at the boy's house. The boy's stepfather did not attend because he was terminally ill. During the conference, the family group learned that the boy, in addition to struggling with the imminent loss of his dying stepfather, had an irrational fear of losing his mother as well. The family came up with a plan for the boy to call his mother every day from the school office to allay his fears. The daily phone call had "a magical effect," according to the school social worker. More support from family members was also offered at the conference, as well as professional intervention, but it was the daily phone calls that turned the tide for the boy, both in coping with his fears during the school day and ultimately with his stepfather's death.

In another case, a high school student was repeatedly truant. He was otherwise well-behaved when he did come to school, but he missed as many days as he attended, and he was sometimes gone for days at a time. His parents, who were divorced, both attended the conference, as well as the student himself, a teacher and some school friends. Everyone had a chance to speak about how he or she was affected by the boy's truancy. At a certain point everyone left the room except the boy, his mother and his father, and they formulated a plan for how the boy would improve his school attendance.

Unfortunately, not every conference achieves the desired results, although overall the outcomes are remarkably productive. In this truancy case, the boy still skipped school at times, despite the best efforts of the parents and the school staff. Nonetheless, the conference produced some benefit. The principal of the school reported that she had an improved relationship with the parents of the truant child. In the next chapter we will further discuss the value of restorative practices — even when they don't achieve the desired outcomes.

This concludes our description of the Restorative Practices Continuum. From informal to formal, these practices are connected by the common thread of affective statements and affective questions — the most basic restorative interventions that are inherent in the more formal interventions. Formal conferences take more time and are used to deal with more serious or complex problems. Impromptu conferences and circles, as well as the individual use of affective statements and questions, achieve positive results without the need for the elaborate preparation associated with formal conferences. They are practical, time-efficient strategies for use on a daily basis. Before concluding this chapter, we would like to discuss how educators may use a restorative attitude to get students to respond positively to all types of restorative practices.

Overcoming Resistance

At first, students may be awkward or reluctant in their response to restorative interventions and practices, especially when these practices are first introduced in a school. Educators should view this apparent resistance as being based in fear rather than belligerence.

Students often find it intimidating and feel vulnerable when they speak on a personal basis and express feelings to each other and to adults in the school. In truth, most adults also struggle with openly expressing their true thoughts and feelings. So our response to student resistance should anticipate this difficulty and be calculated to reduce stress rather than increase it.

Teachers have a wide variety of tools they already use with their students. They probably have never thought about them as "restorative," and maybe they've never thought about them at all. We suggest that one of the lessons of restorative practices is to first become consciously aware of the techniques good teachers use intuitively or occasionally and then use them consciously and strategically — on purpose, all of the time.

One technique is to be upbeat. Greet students as they come into your room in an overtly friendly way. If they seem grumpy or tired as a group, keep saying hello cheerfully until a smile appears on their faces and they answer you back. If a student seems particularly down, you might approach the student quietly and ask if anything is wrong, or if there is something the student needs in order to have a good day in class or in school.

We can also use humor, although we must be strategic and never use it at a student's expense. A counselor in one of our CSF Buxmont schools loves to sing. With one particular student, she uses a song every time he begins to act in a way that she knows is going to lead him into trouble. She flamboyantly sings, with dramatic hand motions, "Stop, in the name of love!" He always laughs at her exaggerated performance and it triggers a positive change in his behavior. He recognizes that her humorous act is helpful to him. That understanding has led naturally to discussions about why he acts the way he does and what he can do when he is struggling with feelings to be appropriate and not hurtful to others or himself.

Another student at a CSF Buxmont school who lacked self-control frequently became angry and caused disruption. Using his desire to be included in an upcoming field trip to an amusement park, the staff asked him to make commitments about controlling his behavior in the time period leading up to the trip. During the trip, the boy rode on the roller coaster with one of the teachers. He laughed harder than the teacher had ever seen him laugh, and they ended up riding together several times on the roller coaster. Back in school, whenever the boy started to act inappropriately, the teacher changed the mood by making a reference to the roller coaster ride. It became a cue for the boy to get a grip on himself and his behavior, so that he could appropriately resolve whatever was frustrating him.

Students can help each other in finding creative solutions. If you ask a student, "How do you think your behavior affects people?" and she says, "I don't know," say to her, "Why don't you go ask some of your classmates and report back to me at the end of the class?" Or, if you're conducting a circle and a student says he doesn't know how to repair the harm, ask the other students what they think. In these ways you avoid an impasse or confrontation when "the questions don't work," and you tap into the creative energy and the relationships that students have with one another.

You can also empower students this way. One of our CSF Buxmont schools asked students to help solve the problem of the school being extremely short-staffed one day. Being a small school, a few teacher absences can potentially have a substantial negative impact on the school environment. So the remaining staff had everyone form a circle and asked the students what should be done. Two of the students loved cooking and were interested in going to culinary school. They suggested that this would be a perfect day for them to make breakfast for the whole school. Some students helped the two do the shopping and cooking while others watched a movie. What might have been a difficult day turned into a positive and rewarding experience for the two student chefs and the other students who demonstrated responsibility and support for the staff.

A common problem that can be addressed restoratively is when you have two students who, as individuals, are a pleasure to have in class. But when they get together, they get into trouble. Instead of arbitrarily imposing a solution to separate them, a restorative approach would engage the two students in solving the problem. Ask them why they like each other, what goals they would like to see each other achieve, what concerns they have for each other and what they think they could do to support each other to achieve those goals. If you raise their consciousness and share the problem, you may be surprised to see how remarkably responsive and resourceful these students can be.

Similarly, if a teacher is hassled by a student who thinks she knows it all and wants to be in charge, then allow that student to teach a class or part of a lesson. Have her prepare a presentation on a topic and deliver it to the class. Let her be responsible for disciplining the students and keeping them focused, while you sit in her seat and either cooperate, or if you think it would be useful, show the student how inappropriately she acts toward you. The reversal of roles will be funny and memorable and is another way of sharing your humorous side with the students. Whichever way you handle the experience, the student will gain some perspective on the challenges of your role and will probably be more open to hearing your concerns about her attitude in class.

Although we can provide examples and suggestions, ultimately you will have to find out which restorative strategies work for you. A staff member at a CSF Buxmont school expressed his own realization about being restorative. He said: "When you do use the restorative process, it never comes across as being fake or phony. It just comes across as being caring. When you do restorative practices consistently, it simply becomes the way you function all the time. It becomes the most natural way for you to relate to people. You don't have to stop and think, 'What should I say in this moment?' You just do it. And when you don't do it, that's when things tend to blow up in your face. It's because you're not using the restorative process."

Restorative Practices and Discipline

Chapter 2
Restorative Practices and Discipline

A trainer for the IIRP was consulting at an urban elementary school when a fight broke out in the cafeteria. The principal called him into the office and asked if he could help. The fight involved two fourth graders who were slapping each other. They had been separated by the staff and were now starting to calm down. The principal wondered if a restorative intervention was possible.

The trainer said to the principal, "Do you have to suspend these students?" She said, "Yes, if we call what happened a fight." But the school was located in a rough neighborhood, and she didn't see any benefit in sending the boys home for the day. She said she had some leeway, as long as she could be convinced that it would be safe for them to stay in the building.

The trainer and two teachers in the school, who were being trained to do restorative interventions, met with the two boys one at a time. They framed the situation by saying to the boys: "The question at hand is whether you are safe enough to be here. We need to know that ultimately you are not going to hurt yourselves or anybody else. The principal has said she will send you home unless you can prove you can stay here. Are you willing to do that?" Both boys said they were.

The next step was to talk to each of the students about the incident itself. The trainer and two teachers asked each of the boys the restorative questions described in Chapter One. Although the boys struggled somewhat, each of them individually talked about what had happened and about how they thought they had affected others. Finally, the teachers said that in order to convince the principal that the boys would be safe, the two boys needed to meet with each other to discuss the incident and come up with a plan for to stop the fighting.

When they all sat down together, the adults asked the restorative questions again, now with the boys sitting together. The two boys were, in effect, both victims and offenders, so they each had a chance to respond to both sets of questions.

Apparently the two had been having a conflict for a long time. When asked, "How has that been for you?" they both talked about how hard it had been to keep the conflict going and that it was a tremendous weight on both of them. They said things like, "I'm so tired of it" and "I'm exhausted." The staff learned, too, that the boys were distant cousins and that the fight had started because of a conflict over a girl. As all these things came to the surface, the boys became increasingly serious and one started to cry. He said tearfully, "I used to be friends with you and I want to be friends again."

The next step was for the boys to come up with a concrete plan. The trainer and the teachers said: "It's not just enough to say you're sorry. We want to know what you are going to do differently." The boys were each given about 15 minutes alone to write down three things they could do to ensure this wouldn't happen again. Once they agreed to and wrote the plan, they were ready to return to class.

Of course, the last time the class had seen the two boys in the lunchroom, they were fighting. Rather than let their fellow students snicker and wonder what happened, they organized a circle to publicly address the situation. The teacher of the class said: "Everybody knows what happened. It was probably pretty scary to see these two boys fighting. But we want everybody to know the great work these two have done." The two boys then told everyone how they talked things through and had come up with a plan to keep from fighting again. The teacher added: "Everybody in this class played into the situation in some way, so now we need to support them in keeping their commitment to avoid fighting. Can you each say one thing you can do to help out these boys?" One child said, "I know I egged you on, but now I'll support you not fighting." Everybody else said something during the go-around. By the end of the circle, the conflict was put to rest, and it has not resurfaced since then.

It might have taken a fair amount of time and effort to work with the two boys and the class. But teachers who use restorative strategies will begin to see each conflict not as an inconvenience but as an opportunity for learning. If you take advantage of these teachable moments, students learn from each other's problems and you begin to use less time and effort to achieve a safe and cooperative classroom. As the story of the two boys' conflict demonstrates, the results can be remarkable.

This chapter focuses on the subject of discipline in general and therefore may seem on the surface to be more relevant to principals, vice principals, guidance counselors and other staff who deal with discipline problems for the whole school. However, many of the ideas presented here will help teachers and other staff to understand different aspects of restorative practices, why and how they work, and how they may be helpful with individuals and in the classroom.

Restorative Practices in Conduct

The role of disciplinarian in a school offers unique challenges. The balance between holding children accountable and creating a positive environment for learning is sometimes difficult to achieve. Demands come from all directions. Teachers want to know "What are you going to do about Johnny?" and "What is his punishment for what he's done?" Johnny may want to be "cut a break" or in some way insulated from the consequences of his behavior. Johnny's parents want "fairness" and a recognition that their child is not like "those bad kids." Is there a way to satisfy these conflicting demands while still meeting the overall needs of the school community?

This chapter will address restorative interventions that can be used by school disciplinarians working with children of any age. There are three key points that need to be addressed first:

1. This chapter will focus on the disciplinarian's role of responding to misbehavior. It will therefore focus on reactive strategies,

although restorative practices are most successful when employed in an environment that implements them proactively as well. Schools that fail to build good relationships and a sense of community will find it more difficult to respond restoratively to problems when they arise. (See Chapter Three, which returns to the issue of creating a comprehensive restorative environment through proactive measures.) The restorative measures described in this chapter are sometimes first employed in discipline for extreme incidents and later filter down to everyday interactions.

2. The IIRP works with schools around the world that operate under different standards, rules, expectations and codes of conduct. This chapter will focus on what disciplinarians can do within their current structures. Restorative practices can be implemented regardless of these differences because they are not a set of rules, but techniques and philosophies that can be applied in any context. Sometimes these practices readily substitute for traditional punitive responses, sometimes not. They may be used as a supplement to existing processes and serve as an additional option. We have tried to describe strategies that can easily fit into existing systems. Still, it is our hope that as educators gain comfort and experience with restorative practices, they will recognize the diminished need for punishment as a response to misbehavior.

3. There is no list of "restorative consequences" in this guide. That is because the list doesn't exist. If it did, we could write common offenses down the left side of the page and corresponding responses to each on the right. However, the very nature of restorative practices makes this impossible. A response that is restorative in one situation could be punitive or permissive in the next. Making a student clean a classroom is a common punishment. Cleaning a classroom might be perfect for a student who had already taken responsibility for making a mess of the classroom, felt bad and wanted to make amends by helping to clean up the mess she caused. But the same punishment (or consequence) might make one student resentful and still another feel like they'd gotten off easy, particularly if the punishment were

perceived as having nothing to do with the misbehavior that led to that consequence.

The nature of the process, not the outcome, makes a response restorative or not.

Social Discipline

The benefits and problems of living in a society constitute a double-edged sword. On the one hand, we benefit from communal activity — trade, education, entertainment, sports, technology and culture. On the other hand, people living together have conflicts. Individuals see things differently from one another or fail to do the right thing or hurt one another. Laws and leaders are supposed to protect groups of people, mediate disputes and maintain order. As a microcosm of society, a school also needs rules and leaders who will carry out those functions. But in the face of increasingly challenging behavior in the form of incivility, misconduct, bullying and even violence, many schools are struggling to fulfill that societal obligation.

Typically we think of the range of possible responses of those in authority to misbehavior on a limited continuum. On one side are the punitive responses, strict and harsh, and on the other side are the nurturing and supportive responses, often labeled as permissive. Your parents, your teachers or other adults you knew as you grew up may have tended toward one end or the other of this "Punitive–Permissive Continuum" (see Figure 4).

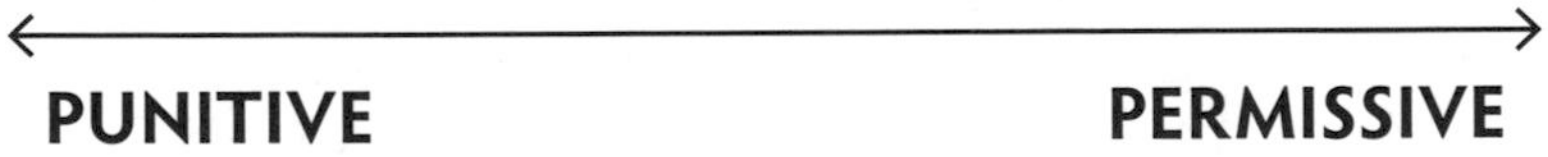

←——————————————————————————————————→

PUNITIVE   PERMISSIVE

Figure 4. Punitive–Permissive Continuum.

The diagram illustrates how our society perceives the possible responses to wrongdoing. If we are not punitive, then we are permissive. There does not seem to be another option. The punitive response, which predominates in today's schools, limits educational authorities to simplistic choices. To punish or not to punish. How much punishment? How many detentions or days of suspension? We assume that a failure to punish will lead to more unruly behavior and is therefore permissive.

In restorative practices we move beyond the single axis of the Punitive–Permissive Continuum. By examining the interplay between two axes, one for "control" or limit-setting and another for "support" or nurture, we discover additional possibilities.

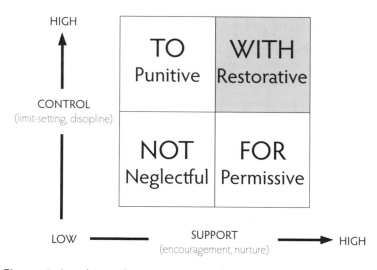

Figure 5. Social Discipline Window.

The "Social Discipline Window" highlights the four resulting combinations (see Figure 5). High control with low support is punitive and high support with low control is permissive. These two combinations mirror the existing simplistic choice defined by the Punitive–Permissive Continuum.

A third response to wrongdoing combines low control and low support. This is the irresponsible or incompetent choice that characterizes a school or classroom where behavior has spun out of control and the adults have abdicated their authority and their responsibility.

The fourth response to wrongdoing combines both high control and high support. This is the critical choice that is missing on the

Punitive–Permissive Continuum. This is when those in authority exercise their control, refusing to accept inappropriate behavior, but do so in a caring and supportive way. This is what we call a "restorative" response to wrongdoing.

The Social Discipline Window suggests that educators or anyone in a position of authority can take the best of both axes and achieve high levels of nurturing and support with high levels of expectation and accountability. The idea is to support students and engage them in finding ways to curb their own negative behavior.

By engaging with young people, we can hold them accountable in an active way. Then we are doing things WITH them. But when we simply hand out punishments, we are doing things TO them. Or when we take care of their problems and make no demands, we are doing things FOR them. And when we ignore their behavior, we are NOT doing anything.

A growing body of evidence suggests that a restorative approach that engages and works with young people is the most effective and beneficial way for schools to respond to wrongdoing. In determining what is restorative, we can assume that the less students are engaged in the process and the less they have to do, the less restorative the approach. The more they are engaged and the more they participate, the more restorative the approach.

To be lectured by the principal or to be given a detention or some other punishment requires no active participation on the part of the student who has misbehaved. In a sense, this is the easy way because it doesn't ask a student to do anything. Ironically, when you are restorative and engage students by asking questions and demanding that they help solve the problem, you will sometimes hear a student say, "Can't you just punish me?" Taking a scrutinizing look at one's own behavior and coming up with solutions to a problem you have created can be very difficult.

So just what are we restoring? We are restoring those who have been harmed by the wrong. We are restoring relationships. We are restoring a sense of well-being and a feeling of community. Unless we accomplish that restoration, conflicts are left unresolved — poised to repeat themselves again and again.

When students are punished, they usually see themselves as victims. They dwell on their own feelings and fail to reflect on the harm they have done to others. Sometimes they are forced to offer an apology, but because they have not had a meaningful exchange with those they have impacted, they lack empathy or insight into others' feelings. Punishment allows offenders to be passive and to avoid real responsibility for what they have done.

Of course, permissive responses also protect young people from responsibility and from facing the consequences of their actions. It is ironic that punishment and permissiveness are so similar in their failure to engage wrongdoers in a meaningful way.

Restorative responses, on the other hand, create opportunities for learning. Restorative processes solicit feelings from teachers, parents, school staff and other students so that an offender can understand the impact of his or her behavior. He or she must also help repair the harm and face up to the true consequences of his or her actions.

The goals of restorative practices that respond to wrongdoing include:

- Trying to foster understanding of the impact of the behavior
- Seeking to repair the harm that was done to people and relationships
- Attending to the needs of victims and others in the school
- Avoiding imposing on students intentional pain, embarrassment and discomfort
- Actively involving others as much as possible

The rest of this chapter will discuss these goals and how restorative practices can be applied in the context of school discipline.

Fostering Understanding

A student had been repeatedly misbehaving on the bus. After several incidents a restorative conference was held. During the meeting the bus driver shared that he was so tired of the problems on his bus that he was considering quitting his job. The student was stunned. He had no idea how his behavior was affecting the driver. Following the meeting, the student caused no more problems on the bus and actually developed a friendship with the driver.

In restorative practices, we start with the premise that students who misbehave are not aware of the impact of their behavior. Even those who behave in ways that appear intentionally harmful rarely understand the true nature and scope of the hurt they are causing. Part of our job as educators is to allow them to learn the consequences of their behavior. That perspective is usually best understood and embraced by educators of students in younger grades. As students get older, teachers come to expect that they will know better and will have already learned these things. This expectation is understandable but not necessarily true.

Each incident of conflict and wrongdoing represents an opportunity for learning. The offending student, those who were directly impacted and everyone else affected by an incident all have an opportunity to share and gain insights and understanding in the wake of what has happened.

Allowing students to better understand the impact of their behavior is more likely to influence their future behavior than the standard sanctions we use in schools. Offending students realize how they have affected other people when they hear directly from those they have harmed. School authorities can achieve this through a variety of means, ranging from informal restorative questions to a more formal circle or restorative conference.

Disciplinarians are sometimes wary about having students and others who have been involved in a wrong or conflict meet face to face to resolve issues, but we have found that this is almost always productive. If we feel concerned about organizing such a face-to-face meeting, we should remember that the individuals in the school who have been involved in a wrong or conflict could meet any time, any place in the school, without the advantage of a supervised restorative encounter. The alternative to a restorative intervention may be a chance encounter with a very negative outcome. Even when all of the parties are not located in the school building, there is the same risk of a chance encounter in the community. Therefore we can conclude that organizing a restorative encounter reduces the risk of further harm.

Repairing the Harm

Someone set fire to a bulletin board in the hallway of a new urban alternative school late in its first school year. Fortunately the damage was minimal, but the smoke alarms were triggered and the school was evacuated.

An administrator at the school called the IIRP for help, saying, "We don't know what to do because we don't know who did it." She was thinking in terms of the traditional questions that schools ask when something goes wrong: What happened? Who is responsible? What punishment do they get? Because she didn't have an answer to the second question, she was immobilized and did not know how to respond to the incident.

We explained to the administrator that she need not know who did what. She could organize a restorative response that would produce useful results, even if she did not catch the culprit. We recommended a restorative circle organized around three restorative questions: What happened? What harm resulted? What needs to happen to make things right?

We explained: "Instead of thinking about the 50 students who attend the school as potential offenders, realize that you actually have, except for one or two actual offenders, 48 victims, all of whom were frightened by what happened, plus yourself and the rest of the school staff, who were also victimized. You're rightfully angry, and you would like to find out who did this. But think about the problem from the victims' point of view. You have all had your day disrupted and your lives put in danger. What do you need to feel safer? There will be value in all of you exploring the restorative questions, even if you don't know who did it."

The school administrator decided to run the restorative circle with the staff and students. When she started, four students refused to participate. They thought the idea of the circle was stupid. Wisely, the administrator avoided a power struggle and instead offered them a deal. She said: "You can sit outside the circle and just watch. But you must each give me your solemn promise you won't disrupt the circle by talking, making faces, laughing or whatever. If you agree, I'll let you sit silently outside the circle." Each student individually agreed to her terms and seated himself or herself on the perimeter.

The administrator had followed our advice in getting a couple of students with whom she had good relationships to promise to speak first and respond seriously. When she posed the questions, her two allies set a good example for the rest. The questions were: "How did you feel about what happened?" and "How were you affected?" The students were very honest and talked about how they "weren't cool with what happened." Some of them said: "Why don't you write on the walls instead? Don't burn the building down." Everyone had feelings about the incident, even though no one seemed to know who had started the fire.

By the time they were on their third go-around, the room was needed for another activity. The administrator moved the group to another room. When they reconvened, the four students who had originally refused to participate asked to join the circle. They saw that the event was not stupid, but in fact was very important, and they wanted to express their feelings as well.

Although the arsonists were never caught, one may assume that if they were students, they were surprised to hear all that anger and fear from their peers. They also heard their peers promise to stop anyone if they saw something like that happening again. So the circle provided an opportunity to redress the harm done, to alleviate feelings and to develop a plan to prevent a reoccurrence. The whole school, including the administrator and staff, had a chance to support each other and affirm a sense of community in the wake of a crisis.

Typical school discipline practices respond to wrongdoing by focusing on the rules that were broken and seek to assert the school's authority by administering punishment to those who broke the rules. While schools do have legitimate authority, we need to remind ourselves that the underlying rationale for school rules is to protect people from harm and ensure a safe and functional learning environment. Rather than a bureaucratic perspective that simply metes out punishment for violations of the code of conduct, our focus should be on the real needs of human beings. We must repair the harm done to interpersonal relationships and restore a feeling of security and peace in the school community, which then makes it possible for teachers to teach and students to learn.

Reparation of harm generally falls into two categories: concrete reparation and symbolic reparation, or a combination of the two. Concrete reparation is repairing or replacing something tangible: returning a stolen calculator or repainting a graffitied wall. Symbolic reparation is saying or doing something that acknowledges feelings, demonstrates remorse or restores peace and harmony. Symbolic reparation frequently involves apology, but apologies can be tricky, so they will be dealt with in more detail in the next section.

Reparation should stem from the desire to make things right. A student who defaces school property might work with the building custodian to repair the harm she has caused and to gain a better understanding of how that person has been affected by her actions. But when an authority arbitrarily assigns a student to do cleaning or some other form of "community service" without a process that fosters understanding, the student is not motivated by a desire to makes things right and merely sees the work as punishment. Even a creative task that might have some inherent learning opportunity for the student, but which was determined without a restorative process, can produce the usual resentment associated with a punishment.

Ideally, students have a say in how they will make things right. That doesn't mean they get to suggest easy or ridiculous solutions. But as part of a restorative process in which a student accepts responsibility, students usually are very helpful and sincere in suggesting a way of repairing the harm and often are tougher on themselves than others are. In those cases where a student is resistant, the authority or the conference participants may indeed choose to impose a punishment. But the more likely and preferable outcome is for students to play a part in making things right. The following example questions can be helpful to students thinking about reparation:

- What can you do to fix this?
- How do you think you could demonstrate that you are sorry?
- Obviously Naomi is pretty upset. Do you have any ideas on how you could make it up to her?
- Your misbehavior was very public. What can you do to show everyone that you feel badly about what you did?
- What you did affected the whole school. I feel like you owe something to everyone. What can you do to settle that debt?

Students will often respond to these questions by saying, "I don't know." Our experience has been that some students might even say: "I don't know. Can't you just suspend me?" This is a clear indication that students usually find it easier to just get punished. The questions represent a significant challenge for them and move them from a passive to an active role — toward authentic accountability.

Often students truly do not know how to respond. They may never have had to think about these kinds of questions before. It is important that the questioner does not fall into the trap of giving them the answers. Instead try some of these responses:

- I know you don't know, but take a guess.
- If you did know the answer, what would you say? (It's funny how often this simple twist of perspective produces a positive result.)
- Who else can you ask for suggestions?
- Pick two other students who will sit with you at lunch today and ask them for suggestions. Come back to me after lunch with the suggestions.
- If you were me, what would you want a student in this situation to do?

Apologies

Apologies are tricky. We often ask students to make them — to teachers, to other students, to staff and to administrators affected by an action. But insincere apologies may actually cause more harm than they repair.

"Say you are sorry!" does not work. Assigned apologies feel hollow to the recipient and foster resentment in those forced to apologize. Repeated verbal apologies with no changes in behavior are equally ineffective. Students need to recognize that apologies with words are meaningless when they are not coupled with apologies of action. Rather than telling a student, "Say you are sorry," ask a question:

- What can you do to make things right?
- Is there anything you want to say to her?
- What do you think would help him feel better?
- If this had happened to you, what would
  you want to have happen now?

Of course, as educators, there will be times we will receive apologies from students. It is important to recognize our own issues, including the fact that apologies are sometimes difficult for us to accept because we may still have negative feelings and perceptions about an incident. So you are likely to have a range of responses — from acknowledgement to a conditional explanation:

- Thank you.
- I appreciate you saying that, and I will feel better
  when I see your behavior change.
- To be honest, I've heard this from you before, but things
  haven't gotten better. I'm glad you are apologizing, but I'm
  going to need something more from you than "I'm sorry."

Undoubtedly one of the most effective ways for students to become confident and competent in making apologies is for them to see them modeled by teachers and administrators in the school. Students need to see that everyone makes mistakes and can make things right. It's simply part of being a good member of the community. When you as an authority figure publicly admit a mistake, apologize for it and follow through on your promise not to make the same mistake again, students will notice and be able to follow your example.

Attending to Needs

A substitute teacher came to the principal very upset that the boys in a class where he was teaching had demeaned him and called him racist names. The principal decided to organize a circle and had one of the staff run the event. The teacher had an opportunity to tell the students (who were middle-school age) how he was hurt by what they had said. The students were very apologetic. The substitute teacher realized that some of the students didn't even understand the meaning of some of the words they had used. He accepted the young people's apologies and trusted that nothing like that would happen again with those students. When one of the students began to cry, the substitute teacher, who by then had had a chance to express his emotions and have them acknowledged, put his arm around the student who was crying and comforted him. The teacher no longer felt victimized and could then move into a helping role. He later told the principal that the circle was the best experience he'd ever had as a substitute teacher.

People affected by misbehavior have needs that must be met. The following is a list of typical needs expressed by victims:

- An opportunity to express emotions
- Acknowledgment from loved ones and colleagues
- Assurance that what happened was unfair and undeserved
- Seeing the offender held accountable
- Financial restitution
- Possible contact with the offender:
  - Apology
  - Having questions answered
  - Assurance of safety

Not every person and not every offense will require that all of these needs be met, but these are some common needs of victims in a variety of circumstances. Of course, the best way to discover what people need is to simply ask them.

A girl's iPod was stolen. She went to the principal about it and the principal asked her, "What do you want to do about this?" The principal didn't leap into the role of investigator, nor did she speculate on the likelihood of finding the stolen item. Rather, she asked the student what her needs were. The student said, "I don't know," so the principal added, "Well, if you had stolen someone's iPod, what would you need to hear in order to want to give it back?" The student decided that she wanted to tell her classmates what had happened and how she felt about it. Among other things, she told them that she had a feeling that she couldn't trust her classmates and that it was a terrible feeling to have. One boy said he thought he might know who took the iPod and that he would talk to that person privately. Later in the day the iPod reappeared.

In another incident, a father articulated a student's needs to the school's administration. He angrily reported to the school principal and counselor that several boys had taunted his son, calling him "gay" and "loser." The boy told his parents that he didn't want to come to school anymore, and subsequently the parents discovered cut marks on their son's wrists. The father said this was having a huge negative effect on his whole family. He said that they had already removed their son from his previous school because of bullying. The boy's father was furious and said he wanted to reprimand the children who were doing this. After having the chance to tell his story, the father agreed to let the school try and sort things out.

The principal and counselor asked the boy if he would agree to a restorative meeting with the boys concerned, acknowledging that this would require some courage. Once the process was explained to him, he agreed. The bullied boy spoke first. He explained the misery he had endured, how alone and hurt he felt, and how school had become a place he no longer wanted to be. As he spoke, the other boys listened intently but with their heads bowed.

Knowing that at least one of the "bullies" had been subjected to the same kind of harassment during the previous year, the counselor asked the boys if they knew how it must have felt to be teased. One of the boys talked about how it had been for him when he'd been called "gay" by other students in a hurtful cyber-bullying incident. Then another boy blinked back tears and spoke in a choked voice of how, in second grade, his teacher had called him a loser and told him he'd never amount to anything. The incident had stayed with him for five years. By the time the boys came to talk about how they could make things right, their bravado was gone and there was a new openness between the boys. After the meeting, the victimized boy reported that he was much happier at school.

One of the surprises that occurs when people have an open forum to safely express their feelings is that the participants benefit in ways that cannot be anticipated. The immediate problem in this case was to stop the bullying and begin to repair the harm that was done to the boy who was being bullied. The unintentional result was that the bullies themselves got to talk about when they had been mistreated and thereby had a chance to resolve some of their own negative feelings and insecurities.

Teachers, in particular, are frequently ignored as victims. While educators are expected to handle incidents professionally, they also have a right to feel safe and valued. When administrators acknowledge teachers' feelings and give them some say in how things will be dealt with, teachers feel trust and satisfaction. Requiring offending students to talk directly to staff who were harmed not only fosters understanding on the part of the students but also assures the adults that things are being taken seriously.

A new teacher had a trick played on her by several students. Instead of going to their next class, they returned for a second period and said they were different students. This happened a couple days in a row, and the students' second-period teacher reported to the principal that the new teacher was allowing the students to stay a double period without her permission. When the principal spoke to the first teacher, it immediately became clear what the students were doing. The teacher, somewhat reluctantly, also admitted that she had been confused. She had returned to teaching after having had a minor stroke. When the students returned to the class saying they were other students, she feared she was really losing it. She was relieved this wasn't the case. Before her next class, the principal helped the teacher form a circle, and the teacher said: "There's some information you don't know. If you knew about it, you wouldn't think what you were doing was so funny." She told them about the stroke. The kids immediately apologized, said they really liked the teacher and promised that they would never do it again.

Punishment

Schools and societies have come to the conclusion that if those who misbehave or commit crimes are made to suffer with a punishment, they will be less likely to repeat the harmful behavior. If this were true, then the job of the school disciplinarian or the criminal court judge would be easy. With each infraction, he or she would impose a certain amount of discomfort. If that punishment failed to change an offender's behavior, then the disciplinarian or judge would simply increase the level of suffering until the inappropriate behavior stopped.

The belief that punishment changes behavior is the basis for school discipline policies around the world. Yet the belief is not supported by evidence. Punishment works only superficially, primarily when the misbehaving students are in view of those in authority. But punishment does not create empathy in students and encourage them to internalize a commitment to behave properly, so as soon as they are out of sight the inappropriate behavior surfaces again. When we punish students by excluding or humiliating them, they do not feel connected to school administrators, teachers or their well-behaved peers. Rather, they feel alienated and instead seek out and bond with others who have been excluded from the mainstream, creating their own negative subculture in the school.

The most significant shortcoming of punishment strategies is that they stigmatize students and label them as "bad." While schools cannot condone and must confront inappropriate behavior, they must do so in a way that allows offending students to reclaim their good name and rejoin the school community. Shedding the "bad student" label and returning to the fold is critical for misbehaving students, if we hope to help young people change their future behavior. John Braithwaite, the distinguished Australian criminologist, who will be discussed below, says that we must "separate the deed from the doer." We should firmly reject the behavior but not reject the person.

In our CSF Buxmont schools and group homes, we have seen the wisdom of this maxim time and time again. Our students, who in the past had been punished, shamed and humiliated in one school after another, continued to behave in ways that brought them more shame and humiliation. Stigmatization, exclusion and alienation serve to perpetuate negative behavior. If we relied on punishment at CSF Buxmont, we would fail miserably in our efforts to help young people change their behavior.

So in the CSF Buxmont schools and group homes, the staff treats young people with a history of negative behavior quite differently. When a student comes through the doors of one of our programs, he or she is greeted by staff who use a restorative approach to respond to problems. Instead of viewing these young people as misfits or outcasts from the public schools, we look at them as good people making bad decisions. We assume that change is possible and that the young people themselves must take responsibility for bringing about that change. Rather than dole out punishments, a strategy that keeps young people in a passive role, the teachers, counselors and house parents engage wrongdoers in solving problems and curbing their own inappropriate behavior. These young people are not allowed to be passive but must suggest their own solutions. We demonstrate respect when we ask a young person to strategize how they can achieve better behavior and

how they can repair the harm they have done to others. Their repara-
tive actions and apologies allow them to feel pride. They are no longer
merely objects of our anger and disapproval but full-fledged human
beings who are capable of making things right. They regain their self-
esteem and move beyond their offender label.

People respond in the same manner that they are treated. If
students are categorized as "bad kids" and alienated from the mainstream, they will continue to fulfill their designated role. But if you
treat young people as having the power to change their bad behaviors,
they frequently avail themselves of that opportunity. The empirical
evaluation of four thousand delinquent and at-risk youth who have
participated in CSF Buxmont's programs over a seven-year period
has produced compelling results. Their likelihood to commit criminal offenses after discharge is more than halved, when compared to
offending rates before participation in our restorative programs. The
evidence affirms that restorative practices curb negative behavior far
more effectively than punishment.

Active Involvement

A high school held an end-of-year pep rally in the gymnasium. It
was an annual tradition, where the seniors passed the torch to the junior
class, and the freshman class-to-be, eighth graders from the middle
school, were invited to the event to be welcomed to their new school.
In the middle of the event, unannounced, a senior star basketball
player suddenly entered the gym wearing only Speedo swim trunks,
body paint and a mask depicting the school mascot. He ran across the
floor and did a very dangerous acrobatic stunt to great applause from
the student body. But the administration was shocked. Although the
boy had never been in trouble during his four years at school, they felt
that the stunt was outrageously risky and could have resulted in great
harm to the student and great trauma to everyone who was watching.
The administration did not want to condone this behavior.

The student was escorted from the gym, the police were called
and the boy was arrested for disorderly conduct. Many students were

outraged by his arrest. When the eighth graders were introduced, normally to be welcomed by applause, they were booed. Subsequently that day the popular student was given further consequences: He was suspended from school for the remaining days of the school year and, while he would be given his high school diploma, he was barred from attending the commencement.

The next day many students arrived at school wearing homemade T-shirts declaring their support for the student. The school administration feared there would be an embarrassing protest of some kind during the graduation ceremony. The assistant principal of the school called the IIRP's training and consulting division for advice on how to deal with the situation. The assistant principal reported that the school administration wasn't willing to back down on the suspension or barring the boy from commencement, but the administration hoped something could be done to prevent students from causing a scene at graduation. The IIRP consultant asked the assistant principal if he had a good relationship with the student. He said: "Yeah, I love him. He's a great kid. I'm really sorry this has happened, and I don't like that this situation has marred an otherwise great career at this high school." Our consultant said: "Call the student and tell him that. And ask him if he'd participate in a restorative conference."

The assistant principal called the student and said: "I really like you, but I don't like what you did. I don't want this to ruin your career here. But I'm concerned about what's going to happen at graduation. We'll organize a restorative conference if you would be willing to talk to the basketball team and some of the likely leaders of the potential commencement protest."

The student agreed. A number of students from the basketball team, the boy, his mother, the principal and other student leaders were present. The discussion was conducted on multiple levels. The principal expressed his anger about what had happened and the students heard this. But the students replied, "He's been a leader at the school for four years, now he's stricken from the record." They asked if they could do a cheer for him at the graduation, but the principal refused this. The student himself felt bad about what had happened. He said to his peers: "I'm getting my diploma. I deserve this punishment. I don't want you to do anything." Finally the valedictorian, who was present at the conference, said: "In my speech, I'm going to mention different people and things they've done during high school. Can people clap when I say his name?" The principal said, "Sure."

The boy made it clear that he didn't think it was in anyone's best interest for the students to do anything other than clap. At the end of the circle, the boy's mom hugged the principal. One might not expect this outcome, but she saw that the principal really liked her son. She realized that the administrators were able to separate her son's inappropriate actions from his worth as a person, and she felt good about the outcome of the conference. After the meeting, word spread from the student leaders to the rest of the student body, and the graduation ceremony took place without incident.

Disciplinarians shoulder the burden of "fixing" things when they go wrong in schools. Rarely do we choose a course of action that equally satisfies the students, teachers, parents and other administrators. Actively involving those most directly affected not only meets their needs better than traditional responses, but it also creates a collective responsibility for fixing things. For many school administrators, shifting from the role of imposer of rules and problem solver to the role of facilitator may be difficult, but it will prove satisfying and productive. In many of the stories in this book, including the one above, good solutions come from students themselves or their parents, not just the school authorities.

One administrator reflected: "I have always prided myself on having the right answers. My combination of assertiveness, creativity and quick thinking has allowed me to deal with issues from minor spats to schoolwide crises in efficient ways. However, operating as the gatekeeper at the revolving door that was my office rarely afforded me the opportunity to reflect on the overall impact I was having on individuals and the school as a whole."

Active involvement of stakeholders takes practice, but it leads to better results. In a high school hallway a girl was yelling at a boy. The boy planted his finger firmly against her forehead, right between the girl's eyes. The girl wasn't hurt, but she was shocked and humiliated, and a loud argument ensued. Security personnel were called to deal with the students, and their parents were called to promptly take them home. Both students were going to be immediately suspended, but everyone hoped this situation could be resolved.

The emotional argument apparently stemmed from the girl's jealousy about the boy dating another girl. When the parents arrived, one of them said, "I'd like to talk to the other parents and work this out." The principal suggested the possibility of a restorative conference, but he was fearful that the parents would antagonize each other and the situation would escalate. "Parents sometimes justify their kids' behavior, and we can't have that," he said. But the parents assured him that they would cooperate, so a conference was immediately convened. The participants included the boy and girl, their parents, the sister of the boy, the principal and assistant principal, and the director of education, who also had a relationship with the boy. The parents, through the conference format, had a chance to talk to each other, and everyone gained an understanding of where each was coming from. They resolved the issues and the two students agreed they weren't going to get in trouble over this any more. The principal offered a "double or nothing" consequence. He said: "If nothing else happens, there will be no suspension. But if you have any conflict again, all the paperwork is prepared and we'll do a double suspension." There were no future conflicts.

In this case, the school — which had involved parents in restorative processes in other instances — was not even thinking about doing a restorative process. But when the parents suggested it, the principal embraced the idea and framed the discussion, and a resolution was reached. The story shows that people often want to be involved and suggests that restorative processes should be a routine option.

School authorities do not have to view their job as having all the answers. Rather, all they have to do is raise the right questions. We need to trust that those most involved in a conflict or wrong have the ability to come up with solutions that will work to solve problems. That doesn't mean that administrators will have no input. But by making conflict resolution a collaborative process, all the stakeholders feel they have contributed, and they are more likely to take ownership and responsibility for successful outcomes.

The Nine Affects and the Compass of Shame

We have talked about how affective questions and statements and other restorative processes provide opportunities for people to express themselves. The psychology of affect, based on the work of psychologist Silvan Tomkins, helps us better understand why human beings act and respond in certain ways and why restorative practices work so well.

According to Tomkins, human beings have nine innate affects (see Figure 6), which can be thought of as the biological basis for our emotions. Each affect is experienced within a range from mild to strong. Two of the affects, interest–excitement and enjoyment–joy, are positive. Surprise–startle is a neutral affect, and its impact is analogous to a restart button on a machine, clearing our mind of whatever we were thinking and allowing it to focus on whatever comes next. Six affects are negative: shame–humiliation, distress–anguish, fear–terror, anger–rage, disgust and dissmell. Disgust and dissmell (a word that Tomkins invented) are not expressed as a range but are distinctive reactions to a bad taste or a bad smell that direct us to expel or avoid whatever is causing the negative reaction.

Donald Nathanson, a psychiatrist who built on and extended his mentor Tomkins' work, has focused his attention on the affect of shame–humiliation. In his book *Shame and Pride* (1994), he explains Tomkins' perspective that there seems to be no specific chemical or electrical triggers for shame, as there are for the other affects. Instead, shame is defined quite simply as the reaction to any interruption of a positive affect.

This definition is often puzzling to a newcomer to the psychology of affect. But it is based on Tomkins' extended observations of

Figure 6. The nine innate affects.

his own children: They looked downward and averted their eyes in shame whenever they were interrupted while enjoying or showing interest in something. These minor instances of shame helped Tomkins realize that shame does not occur just when you do something wrong, but whenever your positive affects are interrupted. In a much more serious context, this perspective helps explain why victims of crime experience a sense of shame when they did nothing wrong, having simply experienced a dramatic and harsh interruption of their positive affects.

Nathanson described four ways in which we react to shame. When something terminates a feeling of interest–excitement or enjoyment–joy in us, the shame that takes place points us in one of the four directions described on his "Compass of Shame" (see Figure 7).

Nathanson observed that when the shame response is triggered, humans respond with "attack other," "attack self," "avoidance" or "withdrawal."

"Attack other" is demonstrated when people blame others for what they've done, turning the tables, lashing out verbally or physically. The example earlier in this book, when a student went into a rage when she received a paper back with a bad grade from a teacher, is a good example of "attack other." She felt shame and lashed out at the teacher when her positive expectation of a good grade was disappointed.

When people put themselves down, saying things like "I'm so stupid" or "Why can't I do anything right?" they are demonstrating "attack self." Some who react to shame by attacking themselves might actually hurt themselves, as in the sad cases of young people who cut themselves.

"Avoidance" usually manifests itself by denial, where a person tries to sidestep a feeling of shame by ignoring it or by changing the subject with jokes or other distractions. In its most hurtful form, avoidance may involve drug and alcohol abuse or thrill seeking as a means to avoid feeling the shame.

"Withdrawal" is exemplified by a student who pulls away or feels she wants to "run and hide." This person may simply clam up when someone tries to talk with her or may withdraw to a private space and refuse to interact with anyone.

Virtually everyone feels or exhibits one or more of these responses every time a positive affect is interrupted. But for most of us, our shame response is mild or short-lived.

Being aware of the Compass of Shame gives us the perspective we need to be restorative when confronting inappropriate behavior. When we call a parent about a child, for example, we need to know that the first reaction of the parent may be to deny and avoid, saying, "He doesn't act like that at home." Or the parent may attack other, turning the tables and blaming the teacher or the school for their child's behavior. Nathanson observed that, in our society, attack other and avoidance are the most frequent responses to shame. Educators should learn to expect these responses when they approach parents.

We can also use the Compass of Shame to examine our own reactions. For example, when we as teachers have put a lot of hard work

Figure 7. Compass of Shame.

into a lesson we think is going to be fun for our students, and then in the first five minutes a student criticizes the assignment or a few kids goof off and disrupt the class, we are going to experience shame. Our positive affect has been interrupted, and we will exhibit one of the four responses on the Compass of Shame. Will we lash out at the students, crawl into a shell, blame ourselves, or try and deny that anything is wrong? It all depends on who we are, but we can be sure that we will experience at least one of those responses. Our awareness of the Compass of Shame allows us to identify our response, react less intensely and quickly recover from our shame response.

We may help people transform and move beyond their shame in a number of ways. When people are experiencing and demonstrating shame, we can:

- Listen to what they have to say
- Acknowledge their feelings
- Encourage them to express their feelings and talk about the experience

Nathanson describes Tomkins' blueprint for emotional health, which states that individuals are at their best when they maximize positive affect, minimize negative affect, express affect freely and do as much of all three as possible. Humans are hardwired to experience all of the affects, so individuals should not prevent themselves or anyone else from experiencing any of the affects, including the negative. However, Tomkins said that it is appropriate for individuals to favor the positive and not dwell on the negative.

Nathanson says that Tomkins' blueprint also fits the relationship of couples. The relationship between two individuals, called intimacy, is best when they agree to help one another maximize positive affect, minimize negative affect, allow for the free expression of affect and do as much of all three as possible.

Finally, Nathanson extended Tomkins' blueprint to community, also at its best when larger groupings of people agree to maximize positive affect, minimize negative affect, allow for the free expression of affect and do as much of all three as possible. This sharing of collective emotions is what makes it possible for restorative practices to improve relationships and transform a school community.

John Braithwaite, the Australian criminologist, in his book *Crime, Shame and Reintegration* (1988), presents another way of looking at relationships and community. Instead of asking the traditional criminological question, "Why do people commit crimes?" he asks instead, "Why do most people do the right thing most of the time?" We could ask the same question about our students — why do most of them behave in school most of the time? Because they want to be thought well of by those people with whom they have a relationship. Braithwaite notes that restorative processes reinforce appropriate behavior by relying on that critical dynamic — our desire to maintain or restore a good feeling with those with whom we have a connection. A judge's lecture is ineffective because the offender has no existing connection to that individual, but a mother's tears are a powerful influence because of the offender's long-standing relationship with that person.

When a person does do something wrong and is confronted with that wrongdoing, the person experiences shame. Braithwaite emphasizes that how we treat the individual is critical. He urges us to "separate the deed from the doer" by acknowledging the intrinsic worth of the person while rejecting the unacceptable behavior. He warns against stigmatizing the offender by labeling him in a way that sustains his sense of shame and alienation. Braithwaite argues that those in authority must allow the offender to restore his relationships by reintegrating him back into society. If an offender cannot restore his relationships, he will seek new relationships with others who also feel alienated from society and join the negative subculture of wrong-doers who see themselves as outside the mainstream.

All the ideas presented above are reflected in the formal restorative conferencing process. During the first part of the conference, when the offender discusses what he has done and people describe their own feelings about the misdeed, the negative affects are expressed freely. The offender experiences shame and usually displays the classic physical response of lowering the head and averting the eyes. As the conference progresses and as feelings continue to be aired, the intensity of the negative affects subsides and the tone of the meeting changes. Positive affects are expressed as the conference moves on to the "making amends" phase. Resolutions are drawn up, and the meeting ends with everyone having refreshments and chatting informally.

The offender and those he has affected all feel better as a result of the opportunity to express emotions freely. As Nathanson's blueprint predicts, the well-being of the community is restored. As Braithwaite predicts, the conference reintegrates the offender by creating an opportunity for him to move beyond his shame, make things right and restore his existing relationships. Interestingly, the conference also often results in the creation of new relationships.

In every situation where students are confronted with the consequences of their misbehavior, whether through a formal conference or a more informal restorative encounter, offenders are likely to demonstrate shame. When a student bows his head and looks down, we need to recognize this as the classic shame response. We should avoid saying, "Look at me when I'm talking," because the student is appropriately showing his shame. Rather, we need to help him move past his shame, create an opportunity for him to make things right and restore his relationship with the school community.

When the star basketball player, mentioned earlier, pulled his stunt in the gym, the administration had him arrested, rupturing his relationship with the school community. By holding a conference where both positive and negative affects were freely aired, even though he was banned from the graduation ceremony, the young man supported the administration and helped prevent embarrassing outbursts from the students. He moved beyond his shame, graciously accepted his punishment and felt reconnected with the school officials, who reaffirmed their positive regard for him as an individual while rejecting his behavior.

Conflict and misbehavior in our schools are inevitable. When educators remember Nathanson's blueprint and strive to create an environment that maximizes positive affect, minimizes negative affect and allows for the free expression of affect, they will transform their schools into true communities, where conflict can be dealt with effectively, relationships can be maintained and learning can occur.

When Things Go Badly

We tend to measure by results, so when we don't immediately get the results we want — the child didn't change his behavior or the problem didn't get fixed — we think we've failed. But this may not always be the case. We may have to step back and look at the picture from a wider or more long-term perspective.

A student dropped a small bag of marijuana that she had hidden in her clothing while on a school field trip. She was invited to participate in a restorative conference to deal with the matter. During the conference she proved to be belligerent and uncooperative. The conference was halted and she was expelled from school.

The judgment could be made at this point that restorative practices did not work in this case. But this was not the end of the story...

Two weeks later the student called the school, begging to be re-admitted. After meeting certain preconditions, such as getting a drug and alcohol–abuse evaluation and following its recommendations, the girl convinced the school administration that she had changed her attitude. She made apologies and commitments about how she would behave in the future. On the basis of these actions, she was re-enrolled. Her mother later commented, "Getting kicked out of the school was the best thing that could have happened." Although the restorative conference itself had not changed her behavior, the overall restorative attitude of the school allowed her to salvage her schooling.

The critical issue is that we always attempt to engage with students and give them opportunities and choices. If a student continues to be uncooperative, you might say: "I'm giving you a chance to be a part of the solution to this problem. If you don't want to help come up with what is going to happen, I'll make a decision for you. But I need you to recognize that you were given the choice." Adopting this kind of posture makes it difficult for students to revel in self-pity or act like victims. They know in their hearts that they were treated fairly and given the chance to participate in a restorative process.

Furthermore, restorative practices, even if they don't seem to help or change the offender, often have a positive impact on other people involved in an incident. With traditional methods of discipline, teachers, staff, parents and other students may be completely neglected. But with restorative practices, they are given a voice and a chance to deal with their feelings.

For example, if a student who has misbehaved refuses to participate in a circle to discuss how he has affected his classmates and is consequently suspended from school, the class and the teacher may still benefit by holding the circle. Talking as a group, they can deal with what happened, discuss how they were affected and come up with ideas for how they might support a fellow student to avoid the same misbehavior. They may even brainstorm ideas for how to repair the harm done, even though the student who caused the problems has refused to be present. Ultimately, if the door is left open and the misbehaving student is treated respectfully and not humiliated, there is always a chance that she will find the strength to make amends at a later time.

Consequences

Generally, we believe that there should be some kind of consequence for misbehavior, that something should happen to a student who has broken a rule, hurt someone or acted out in some other way. Often our trainers are asked whether we think that having a student experience a consequence is important.

The answer is yes, consequences are always appropriate, but consequences need to be differentiated from punishment. While it may sound like semantics, the difference is important. Jane Nelson, in her book *Positive Discipline* (1996), defined a punishment as something that is imposed on someone, generally with the intention of creating pain or discomfort, for an infraction against some authority. A consequence, on the other hand, can be defined as the result or effect of an action or condition, usually a natural or related result. In disciplinary situations, the ideal consequence puts responsibility on the offender.

When a student is caught smoking outside the school by the principal the day before a field trip, he might simply be punished. The principal confiscates the cigarettes, brings the student to his office and says: "You can't go on the trip. In addition to that, while the rest of the class is on the trip, you will stay in the school and write an essay on why it's necessary to follow school rules."

But the principal could instead opt for a consequence to the student's inappropriate behavior that puts more responsibility on the student. In this case, the principal confiscates the cigarettes and brings the student to the office. He says: "You know, your timing is awful. Tomorrow you're going to be on a class trip where there will be very little structure and supervision, and yet I can't even trust you to follow the rules here at school where there's lots of structure and supervision. How can I afford to jeopardize the trip for the other students by allowing you to attend?"

The principal further engages the student. He says, "You have until the end of the day to convince me that I can trust you to go on the trip." The student may ask, "How can I convince you?" The answer might be: "I don't know, but I'll tell you when you succeed in doing so. Why don't you ask some of your friends to help you?"

The outcome may be similar in either case. But in the latter example, a different result is possible if the student can convince the principal that there is some way he can be trusted. The significant difference is that with a punishment the student is passive, having neither power nor responsibility. He resents the principal and thinks he is a victim. With a consequence, the student can be active, has both power and responsibility, and is put in a position where he will be likely to a look at his behavior and reflect on how his behavior has impacted other people.

One of the most persistent myths in school discipline is that punishment is a way of "holding students accountable." But punishment only works when the authority is watching and relies on external control. Restorative methods impose a consequence rather than a punishment and help to create empathy and active involvement. A consequence dramatically improves the chances that positive attitudes and behaviors will be internalized and that young people will behave well, not merely out of fear, but because they want to feel good about themselves and have a positive connection to others.

CHAPTER **3**

Leadership and School Change

Chapter 3
Leadership and School Change

———————————————————

Running a school is a complex task. Learning outcomes, safety, standardized test performance, teacher retention, building maintenance, budgets and strategic plans are only a few of the challenges a school administrator faces. Even with a strong staff, hardworking students and supportive parents, an administrator still has a very difficult job. So the idea of implementing a new program for dealing with unruly students, reaching out to disconnected parents and educating staff with varying degrees of openness to new ideas may seem overwhelming.

The field of restorative practices offers a framework for implementing schoolwide change while at the same time engaging all of the stakeholders. In this chapter we will focus mostly on the idea of change guided by a building administrator, but we recognize that anyone in a school — staff, parent or student — could be an agent of change. A teacher, without necessarily having administrative support or explicit approval, can implement many of the ideas presented in the first two chapters of this book and find great success in transforming his or her classroom. The ideas could even begin to spread to other teachers. However, because a building principal is the only one who has overall authority, meaningful whole-school change will not occur without his or her support and commitment.

David Gleicher's "Formula for Change" (attributed to Gleicher in Beckhard & Harris, 1987) is a helpful way of looking at the possibility of achieving intentional change in a school:

Dissatisfaction + Vision + Practical Approach > Resistance

According to this formula, intentional change is possible when:
- A perceived need for change (often expressed as dissatisfaction with how things are now) and
- A compelling vision of what is possible and
- A practical approach to bringing about those changes (seen as concrete steps that can be taken toward the vision)
- Are collectively greater than the resistance to change.

Perceiving the Need for Change

The schools that approach the IIRP to learn about restorative practices share a common recognition that there is something about their schools they want to change. They may or may not have the words to describe exactly what they're looking for, but the crux of the issue is generally a shared feeling that the sense of community in their school needs to improve.

School administrators vary in how they describe why they are considering the implementation of restorative practices. Many have a desire to simply improve school culture — to have better relationships between students and staff, among students themselves, and between the staff and students' families. Others identify the need for better behavior among their students or for better decorum in classes.

Regardless of how the administrators or staff of a school describe the reason for change, the school as a whole must perceive a need for change. A school need not be facing a crisis to want positive change. For example, one administrator who contacted the IIRP for training said: "We don't have significant discipline problems here. But student interest in extracurricular activities is dropping off, there seems to be a lot of apathy, and we'd like to bring back a sense of school spirit." So the only requirement to get the ball rolling is that people have a desire to make things better.

The Vision of Restorative Practices

Restorative practices is not a one-size-fits-all-schools system for change. Each school must develop a unique vision of what they want to achieve. We urge schools to employ quantitative measures to study the results of restorative practices. Most schools report dramatic reductions in disciplinary incidents. Some schools trained by the IIRP, for example, have reduced office referrals by half in a single year. Other common measures include reductions in administrative detentions, suspensions and expulsions. Incidents of classroom disruption often decline sharply, as well as fighting, smoking, tardiness and absenteeism. (See Abbey J. Porter's "Research Reveals the Power of Restorative Practices in Schools," in *Safer Saner Schools: Restorative Practices in Education*, Mirsky & Wachtel [Eds.], 2008, chap. 19.)

Qualitative outcomes, though more difficult to measure and report, can be even more dramatic. Although to date reporting of qualitative improvement has been largely anecdotal, teachers in schools that have achieved a restorative culture report more positive collaboration between students and teachers and among the teachers themselves. A sense of teamwork develops and people are more inclined to resolve problems through cooperation. Administrators report that their relationships with teachers improve and become more collaborative, rather than strictly supervisory.

Students have also reported that they sense a different school climate in a restorative school than in other schools. For example, a transfer student from a traditional school to a restorative practices school said, "One thing I noticed right way was the friendly atmosphere." Another girl switched from a restorative school to a traditional school. Her mother said to the new principal, "You have a nice school here, but something's missing." She moved her daughter back to the first school. Some time later, the principal of the traditional school investigated what that "something missing" was and eventually adopted restorative practices in her own school.

Familiarity with other schools' success is a way new schools can set goals for the use of restorative practices. Yet each school must articulate its own unique vision of what it would like to achieve.

Organizational Change: A Practical Approach

Once a school recognizes a need for change and articulates a vision for the future, the next step is to set a course for implementation of the desired changes. Of course, sustained change will not happen overnight. It requires an incremental process that is suited to the school.

When the IIRP is invited to a school to discuss restorative practices, we almost always meet first with the school principals, guidance counselors and anyone else responsible for maintaining the sense of culture in the school building. We talk very briefly about restorative practices, but then we ask what the school's needs are.

Often the leadership of the school perceives a crisis, but not always. The principal may say that too many kids are being sent to the office or there are too many disruptions in the classroom. Whatever the school's needs, we always emphasize that while we may be the experts in restorative practices, the administration and staff of that school are the experts in their own building. As trainers and consultants, we can encourage and instill hope. We can provide tools, techniques and new perspectives. Ultimately, however, the school can and must solve its own problems.

Such a participatory approach is a way of modeling the essence of the restorative approach that we advocate, but it is also the plain truth. While teachers and staff can be trained in restorative practices, they have to go and try out what they've learned. More consultations and more trainings are useless without their commitment to take risks and practice what they have learned. That's why we recommend, soon after staff are trained, that the school leadership organize the first of a series of hour-long circle meetings to provide a restorative forum for staff to discuss what restorative approaches are being tried and to tell their stories of success and failure in a comfortable setting. We don't want to offer more training until a school is actually beginning to use the restorative approach. Teachers and administrators learn restorative practices by being restorative and then by reflecting and examining what works, what doesn't and what else can be tried.

Organizational Change Window

The "Organizational Change Window" (see Figure 8) defines the restorative path to change by mirroring the Social Discipline Window. Instead of control and support, the two axes that underpin the Social Discipline Window, the two axes of the Organizational Change Window are pressure and support.

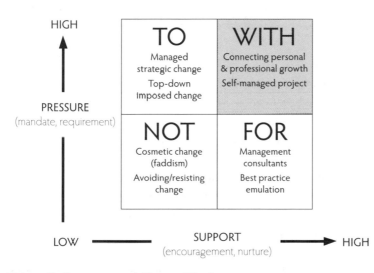

Figure 8. Organizational Change Window.

Change TO people. Pressure without support breeds resentment and resistance. Imposing change from above may seem to be the quickest way to institute change, but without support for the staff and without participatory engagement, change is superficial and fleeting. The top-down method has traditionally been the approach to change in many organizational structures, but we argue that it fails to achieve change that is effective, meaningful and enduring. Like punishment, changes imposed by pressure alone work only when those in authority are watching, but they are not internalized by the organization's staff.

Change FOR people. Support without pressure wastes resources. Providing tools and strategies without ensuring their use rarely brings change. Most people are inherently resistant to change, particularly if they don't perceive a genuine commitment to that change on the part of the administration. Without pressure to back up initiatives, people will ignore new ideas and avoid making changes. It is the rare person who wakes up in the morning and says, "I think I'd like to have some personal growth today." Growth, both personal and professional, needs the leadership's firm commitment as a motivating force to overcome inertia.

NOT doing change. When neither pressure nor support are present, the best that can be hoped for is the false illusion of change. Many bureaucracies demonstrate this pattern. Initiatives are introduced with no support or mandate so the change is merely cosmetic. The proposed change is perceived by everyone in the organization as peripheral to the primary role of the organization and therefore is largely ignored. Staff, who have seen this phenomenon repeated again and again, simply wait for the latest initiative to pass and joke when the next one arrives.

Change WITH people. The most effective way to bring about change in a school — or any organization — is to combine high levels of both pressure and support and engage staff in a participatory process. Real change will occur only when teachers and staff recognize that they will be held accountable for change and simultaneously are given the support and tools they need.

Fair Process

Fairness is an essential ingredient of a successful change process. An excellent article on organizational management that appeared in the *Harvard Business Review* suggested that there are three key components to people's perception that a process was fair: engagement, explanation and expectation clarity (Kim & Mauborgne, 1997).

Fair process simply means that people are treated in a respectful way:

- "Engagement" means that everyone affected by a decision is given the chance to provide input and have an opportunity to discuss various possible courses of action.
- "Explanation" means that after a leader has made a decision, that decision and the process and reasoning behind the decision are made clear to all stakeholders.
- "Expectation clarity" means that everyone involved understands the implications of that decision, the specific expectations and the consequences for failing to meet those expectations.

Fair process does not mean democracy. We are not advocating that a school make decisions by putting them to a vote or by trying to meet every individual's needs. Fair process is about creating open channels of communication and about giving people reason to believe that their ideas and feelings truly have been taken into account. People do understand that a school administration is ultimately responsible for making the decisions it deems fit. But when people feel they have been treated fairly, they are more likely to cooperate willingly with the decisions that are made — even when the outcomes are different from the ones they may have preferred or desired.

When CSF Buxmont schools first introduced the use of restorative conferencing, Ted Wachtel, the founder and executive director at that time, relied on the use of fair process to get the staff's support in accomplishing this organizational change. He told the staff that he had invited several Australians to train them, but that he was not sure how conferencing could best be implemented in the CSF Buxmont schools. He asked for their support and especially their input. He hoped that after the training, some of them would try the process with our students when behavior problems arose. After the trainings, staff freely voiced their opinions, including some who were skeptical. But others went ahead and used the conferencing process.

Wachtel, based on subsequent discussions with staff, decided that in the future, conferencing would be used, in particular, for the most significant incidents, including those that might have otherwise resulted in expulsion from school.

Using fair process, he had engaged staff by seeking their help in trial conferences and by soliciting their opinions. He then explained his decision to implement conferencing in terms of reducing discharges and improving the reintegration of students back into the school community after their disruptive behavior had adversely affected everyone. He also made his expectations clear for the future: that each of the CSF schools should have a few individuals gain experience to serve as conference facilitators so that they would be available whenever appropriate incidents arose.

Restorative conferencing was smoothly implemented into all of the CSF Buxmont schools. Fair process facilitated a change that otherwise might have been adversarial. People felt acknowledged, that their opinions were valued and that, even if their views differed with the decision of the leadership, they supported the decision because they felt that they were treated fairly.

Tips for Working with Staff

When an administration wants to bring restorative practices to a school, the leadership must effectively engage the staff. In the spirit of fair process, teachers and nonprofessional staff must know that they will have some voice in the implementation. Frequently teachers and other staff members will have concerns and questions about restorative practices. A critical element in addressing these issues is to ensure that the staff is informed early in the process. If administrators emerge from a series of closed-door sessions and announce that the school will be adopting restorative practices, fears and resentments will arise and make implementation more difficult. It is far more effective when administrators tell staff early on that they've heard about the restorative approach and that they are looking into learning more about how it could be used in the school.

Typical concerns and questions from staff include:
- I don't have time for this.
- I'm a teacher, not a counselor or social worker.
- Does this mean kids can just apologize and nothing else happens?
- What does this have to do with my subject area?

Teachers must understand that restorative practices can help them do their jobs more easily and more effectively. They will not be asked to become therapists nor to take on more responsibility. Teachers who employ restorative practices experience fewer class disruptions and lose less class time, allowing them more time and a better environment for teaching. Some teachers may need more time than others to recognize the potential effectiveness of restorative practices. In some cases they won't try restorative approaches until they've seen the success other teachers have had using restorative practices in their classes.

One of the first schools to implement restorative practices decided to work in stages, first with the "early adopters," those teachers who were initially most responsive to the idea. In the first year, the IIRP provided a basic understanding of restorative practices for those who were most receptive and taught them to be a support group for one another. One teacher commented on how well that worked for the group. She said that teachers used to complain to each other about students and judge them. Now, they found themselves discussing how to handle a student's behavior and brainstorming as a group about how to respond to different situations more effectively.

By the second year the "fence sitters," those teachers who were not necessarily against restorative practices but who were reserving judgment, began to notice the positive results of restorative practices among the early adopters. They joined the existing group and were also trained. The early adopters modeled restorative practices, provided support and told stories about their experiences, so the fence sitters learned from this as well. By the third year the "resisters," those teachers who continued to hold out for more evidence of the merit of restorative practices, were seeing its value. Those who had been resistant became less so, and some of the most resistant teachers retired. Newly hired teachers were trained with the third group, and finally all the teachers were expected to use restorative practices in their classroom. ("Early adopters," "fence sitters" and "resisters" are terms borrowed from Geoffrey Moore's *Crossing the Chasm*, 1999.)

While it is useful to identify differing degrees of enthusiasm and support for restorative practices among teachers and staff, we do not recommend the staged approach to training used by this pilot program. We believe that it is most beneficial for all teachers to be trained together. When an entire staff is introduced to restorative practices as a whole, everyone can test the waters and participate in discussion at the same time, and the program will have a better chance of gaining credibility more quickly. However, the follow-up support circles should be voluntary, so enthusiastic teachers are not discouraged by resistant curmudgeons. Confidence and momentum will gradually build among the faculty until the most resistant teachers find themselves vastly outnumbered.

The ideal situation, from our perspective, is when nonprofessional school staff, including secretaries, cafeteria workers, custodians, bus drivers and hall monitors, are all included in the initial training. Secretaries, for instance, are the first people to meet a student sent to the office. A secretary can begin the restorative process by asking, "What happened, Bobby?" and "Who do you think was affected by what you did?" This helps set the tone for when the student does speak to the administrator. Another reason for all staff to be trained in restorative practices is to help support the general changes in school culture. These staff will use restorative practices in their daily interactions with students, and they will understand what is happening if they are asked to be involved in a restorative intervention, such as a restorative conference.

Of course, a single day of training in restorative practices is only a first step. The vision for change is long term, so it is necessary to begin the process modestly and find out what needs to happen next.

The tendency may be to think, "How can we change the whole school culture? That seems so difficult," and then feel too paralyzed by the enormity of the vision to do anything at all. We urge administrators, teachers and other staff to avoid feeling overwhelmed by the big picture by simply trying out what they've learned in the first training and reflecting on the experience. As teachers try out restorative practices in their classes, administrators use them in disciplinary situations, and people begin to share their experiences with one another, everyone will get new ideas, and the small results will begin to build. The cumulative effect of staff making small changes here and there will slowly impact the whole school culture. The idea is to start where you are and do what you can. "There's only one way to eat an elephant," said one administrator who helped pioneer restorative practices in his school, "one bite at a time."

Overcoming Teacher Resistance

"In your own classroom you can close the door and do what you want" represents the independence that characterizes many teachers' thinking, but school culture change requires collaboration. While public schools have encouraged cooperative practices, such as team teaching and curriculum mapping, little has been implemented to ensure that the issues of school culture and discipline are handled consistently throughout a school building.

Most educators are uncomfortable about approaching colleagues for suggestions about how to engage reluctant students and deal with minor classroom disruptions. They do not typically share ideas about what is working well in each other's classrooms. When there is discussion, it is all too often cynical or complaining, rather than caring and constructive. Often administrators are too burdened with their own pressing problems to take time to deal with individual classroom management issues. The norm seems to be: "It's your class. Deal with it."

If you look at the big picture, however, these attitudes squander human resources. Schools have hundreds, even thousands, of years of combined experience among their teaching, advising and administrative staff. The expertise in any given building is incredibly rich. Part of working *with* people is tapping into and sharing that experience. We often point out that restorative practices is not new. Good teachers have always been restorative, intuitively engaging their students. But our work in restorative practices brings those good instincts to conscious awareness and makes them explicit so they can be shared and so they are consistent throughout a school — done on purpose, all of the time.

Still, most schools compartmentalize that rich knowledge, history and experience so that it is not shared. There may be two major reasons why this compartmentalization of knowledge persists.

First, most teachers are afraid to admit they need help because they don't want to be seen as ineffective or weak. Leaders have to work to change this belief by making consultation and collaboration a regular part of the business of the school. When we talk about support being a necessary component of restorative practices, that means administrators must create a supportive environment for staff to feel comfortable asking for help and sharing ideas. "Having all the answers" must give way to "creative collaboration," so teachers can be honest and helpful with one another. Restorative practices are not just for the benefit of students.

Secondly, there are typically no systematic opportunities for teachers to sit and talk about these types of classroom issues. Staff and team meetings and in-service days tend to be taken up with other priorities, like academic goals and administrative issues. Teachers are rarely given the opportunity or a safe forum to discuss student behavior. By making behavioral issues a priority, leaders can help teachers help each other. Even regularly scheduled discussions, just an hour every four to six weeks, can go a long way toward opening new lines of communication. Teachers sharing ideas this way helps restorative approaches spread very quickly through a school, as teachers report what has worked and ask for suggestions to deal with various problems.

In one school where there was some resistance to the implementation of restorative practices, a meeting was organized to allow teachers to air their concerns. The meeting began with some teachers expressing that they did not want to be told how to behave in their own classrooms. That created a temporary impasse until one respected teacher, who had been at the school for a number of years, stood up and said, "As teachers here, none of us is in private practice." That statement helped the other teachers move toward recognizing their collective responsibility to create a better school culture. Surprising and positive results occur when teachers who may be initially resistant to the idea of restorative practices take risks and try to use them.

An advanced geometry teacher was having difficulty with a class. He knew something was wrong, but he couldn't understand what it was. The students were not asking questions or completing homework. They seemed uncooperative, yet they were a bright class and normally compliant. The teacher was somewhat uncomfortable with restorative practices but, to his credit, he wanted to see if it could be helpful. He engaged the support of his principal and eventually asked another teacher to facilitate a circle, which he attended as a participant. When the circle was held, the students opened up, and they admitted that they were intimidated by the teacher. They knew he was intelligent and expected a lot, and it made them afraid to ask what they feared the teacher might see as "dumb questions." When they didn't do or turn in their homework, it was because they were afraid to show their mistakes. The circle provided an excellent opportunity for the teacher to hear what his students were thinking and get to know them better. By the same token, his willingness to participate in the circle allowed the students to get to know him better and start to feel more comfortable in his class. After that circle, he took over running circles himself whenever he felt they were needed, and continued to develop a better relationship with his students.

The teacher took a risk. By admitting he didn't have all the answers to what was going on in the class and by asking for help, he was able to use a restorative process to return his class to its primary purpose — for students to learn geometry.

Getting Students and Parents on Board

In addition to staff, students should also be introduced to the general concepts of restorative practices. Even without a formal introduction, students will become aware of the changes in the school culture and how teachers and administrators are interacting with them. However, providing an educational experience for students in restorative practices will help prevent misunderstandings and false assumptions that are likely to arise. In one school, after an initial introduction, teachers were enthusiastic to begin using restorative questions. A week later, the students started asking the teachers, "Why are you all asking us the same questions all of a sudden?" They started giving the answers they thought the teachers wanted to hear. They didn't understand the reasons for the questions.

Students can learn about restorative practices in a number of ways. The restorative concepts can be introduced as English, social studies or health lessons. Or in secondary schools, homeroom teachers can provide an introduction. Since stories help illustrate the points, as they have throughout this book, a story followed by a discussion can be a great way to introduce students to the new ideas. PowerPoint presentations and videos about restorative conferences and other restorative practices in schools and other contexts have been produced by the IIRP and other organizations. These can be shown in a class or assembly of students. Some schools have used their in-house cable system to show a video about restorative practices to the entire student body at once. A simple study guide can be used to raise questions, introduce a variety of related topics and generate discussion between students and staff. The IIRP has also produced workbooks that can be used in individual classes (see Educational Resources at the end of this book).

Parents, too, should be familiarized with the ideas of restorative practices. Generally, a letter home from the principal explaining restorative practices and how students will be impacted can give parents initial information. Schools can also invite parents to information sessions about restorative practices. Getting busy parents to attend may require some thoughtful marketing — making it clear that this is an important development. The same presentations that are given to children can be adapted for parents by explaining that this is how these ideas are being presented to their children during the school day. In some communities, it is possible for a video presentation to be shown on local-access cable television, which has the potential to reach the greatest number of families and others in the community who might have an interest in these ideas. Experience shows that parents are receptive to these ideas and that they appreciate a school's efforts to involve students and their families in improving the school climate.

Of course, the biggest impact on students and parents — as well as teachers and administrators — will come about naturally as restorative practices are implemented and refined in a school. Everyone will get a better feel for what it means to be restorative and how to be restorative. We envision a future where students are trained to facilitate restorative processes. This has already been done with peer mediation, but not often with restorative circles or conferences. Parents may also be selected and trained to serve as facilitators of restorative conferences in schools.

Other Applications

Restorative practices will be most successful in schools where administrators use the practices in their interactions with teachers. Staff meetings can include circle go-arounds. Initially, this activity can be used to introduce some ideas of restorative practices, but go-arounds may also become a regular feature of staff meetings. Go-arounds may allow staff to air concerns, share positive developments and get to know each other better. Such meetings serve as a practical demonstration of the dynamics of circles, and teachers who participate in those staff meetings will have greater appreciation for how this can work in their classes.

One of the basic premises of restorative practices is that human beings are happiest, healthiest and most likely to make positive changes in their behavior when those in authority do things WITH them, rather than TO them or FOR them. This is not just true for people under the age of 18. As your school develops its understanding of restorative practices, there will be opportunities for the staff to benefit from this powerful approach, too. Staff supervision may be conducted restoratively, and restorative meetings can be extremely useful in mediating conflicts that arise among staff members.

The CSF Buxmont schools routinely use a circle format for staff meetings. Working with delinquent and at-risk youth all day is especially challenging and stressful, so having a forum where you can express feelings and work through conflicts with other staff has proved to be amazingly effective in maintaining high morale and effective communication.

Further, administrators may create their own peer groups for hashing out difficult issues. A school principal may sometimes feel isolated and alone, but it is possible for principals from several schools in a district to meet as a peer group and help each other resolve problems. We have also found that when a school district implements restorative practices in one building or part of a building, the word tends to spread, and other teachers and principals become interested in learning more. It becomes easier to replicate the results at other school sites when channels of communication between administrators throughout a school district have already been opened.

Maintaining Momentum and the Need for Self-Assessment

For institutional change to be lasting and effective, as suggested in the Organizational Change Window, the administration has to continually provide both pressure and support. After the initial implementation of a new program, the excitement wears off and other priorities come to the fore. At this point, there needs to be a clear statement from the administration that the shift to restorative practices is still important; otherwise the initiative will fall apart. Regular meetings of staff, perhaps every six weeks, to discuss what's working for them in terms of restorative practices, has proven extremely effective for helping to maintain momentum.

Reflection is critical for an administrator. In an ambitious change process like this, administrators must examine their own behavior, question their assumptions, listen to those over whom they exercise authority, and continually strive to make corrections and improve their own capacity to act restoratively. Every instance of restorative practices implementation of which we are aware, including our own CSF Buxmont schools, has proved to be a challenging learning process for all who are involved. The most restorative school in the world should still seek to refine its practices and find ways to be yet more restorative and less punitive.

At various intervals leaders can ask themselves the following questions:

- Does your school encourage meetings, communication and the drawing up of agreements between those who have done harm and those who have been harmed?
- Does your school provide opportunities for those who have done harm to make reparations and give apologies, and does the school provide the support needed for offenders to make changes?
- Does your school help reintegrate both those who have done harm and those who have been harmed by offering necessary support and assistance?
- Does your school involve all stakeholders in learning about restorative processes, listen to all voices when a wrong is committed, and invite all those affected to participate in restorative meetings?

These four questions (adapted from Van Ness & Strong in Restorative Justice Consortium's *Statement of Restorative Justice Principles: As Applied in a School Setting*, 2005, pp. 14–18) will help you track your progress and answer the questions "How restorative is your school?" and "How restorative can your school be?"

Conclusion

We cannot overstate the potential for restorative practices in schools, but nor should we underestimate the challenges to accomplishing a change of this significance in school culture. Yet the number of schools in various stages of implementation around the world suggests that restorative practices will not be a mere fad, but a transformative movement that promises change for schools around the globe.

We hope that you find this book a useful and practical resource to help you undertake your own restorative journeys in your own classrooms and schools. The International Institute for Restorative Practices is available to help you along your way. Best of luck in your endeavors.

References

Beckhard, R., & Harris, R. T. (1987). *Organizational transitions: Managing complex change*. Boston: Addison-Wesley Publishing Co.

Braithwaite, J. (1989). *Crime, shame and reintegration*. New York: Cambridge University Press.

Kim, W., & Mauborgne, R. (1997). Fair process. *Harvard Business Review*, January 1.

Moore, G. (2002). *Crossing the chasm*. New York: HarperCollins Publishers.

Nathanson, D. L. (1992). *Shame and pride: Affect, sex and the birth of the self*. New York: W.W. Norton & Company.

Nelson, J. (1996). *Positive discipline*. New York: Ballantine Books.

Porter, A. J. (2008). Research reveals the power of restorative practices in schools. In L. Mirsky & T. Wachtel (Eds.), *Safer Saner Schools: Restorative Practices in Education* (pp. 177–192). Bethlehem, PA: International Institute for Restorative Practices.

Restorative Justice Consortium. (2005). *Statement of restorative justice principles: As applied in a school setting* (2nd ed.). Retrieved November 11, 2008, from http://www.restorativejustice.org.uk/Resources/pdf/Principles_Schools_2005_2nd_ed.pdf

Educational
Resources

To learn more about DVDs, books
and other resources offered
by the IIRP, please visit:

store.iirp.edu

Books

Many books are available as eBooks and in other languages.

Restorative Circles in Schools: Building Community and Enhancing Learning
By Bob Costello, Joshua Wachtel & Ted Wachtel

A practical guide to the use of circles in schools and other settings, as well as an in-depth exploration of circle processes. The book includes numerous stories about the way circles have been used in many diverse situations, discussion on the use of proactive, responsive and staff circles, and an overview of restorative practices, with particular emphasis on its relationship to circle processes.

Restorative Justice Conferencing: Real Justice® and The Conferencing Handbook
By Ted Wachtel, Terry O'Connell & Ben Wachtel

Two books in one volume: (1) the official training manual that provides a step-by-step guide to setting up and conducting restorative conferences and (2) actual stories to show how conferencing works and how it can change the way our society responds to wrongdoing in schools, criminal justice, the workplace and elsewhere.

Family Power: Engaging and Collaborating with Families
By Elizabeth Smull, Joshua Wachtel & Ted Wachtel

Practical guidance for engaging and collaborating with families, illustrated by anecdotes gathered from professionals in a range of settings around the world. The authors connect FGC/FGDM with the broader field of restorative practices, which holds that "people are happier, more cooperative and productive, and more likely to make positive changes when those in positions of authority do things *with* them, rather than *to* them or *for* them."

Building Campus Community: Restorative Practices in Residential Life

By Joshua Wachtel & Ted Wachtel
(opening chapter by Stacey Miller & Ted Wachtel)

A practical handbook on the use of restorative practices in campus residential life. The authors provide comprehensive implementation guidelines as well as numerous stories — some enlightening, some comical, some poignant — about how the practices are being applied in higher education. The practices can foster positive relationships, respond to conflicts and problems, and raise consciousness about bias, alcohol abuse and other critical campus issues.

Forging Justice

A "restorative justice mystery" by Margaret Murray

In her search for three girls who robbed a convenience store and beat the owner into a coma, Detective Claire Cassidy meets high school vice principal Daniel Pierce. Frustrated by a system that too quickly throws kids out onto the street, Pierce claims he knows a better way. Claire decides to put up with him just long enough to find her suspects. But as they work together in what may be her last case, Claire begins to see that Pierce's methods may have merit both in her work as a cop and in helping her confront personal trauma from her past.

Dreaming of a New Reality

By Ted Wachtel

A practical guide to the use of circles in schools and other settings, as well as an in-depth exploration of circle processes. The book includes numerous stories about the way circles have been used in many diverse situations, discussion on the use of proactive, responsive and staff circles, and an overview of restorative practices, with particular emphasis on its relationship to circle processes.

DVDs

Many of our DVDs include English subtitles. Several have subtitles in other languages.

Beyond Zero Tolerance:
Restorative Practices in Schools

25 minutes

A powerful testament to the benefits of restorative practices in an educational setting, this film documents implementation in several schools in the U.S., the Netherlands, and Hull, England. The camera captures circles, conferences and one-on-one meetings in progress. Students, teachers and administrators speak candidly about the effects of restorative practices in their school. The viewer is transported to bustling school hallways and classrooms and feels an unmistakable sense of lively and cheerful community.

Burning Bridges

35 minutes

A documentary about the arson of Mood's Bridge, a historic covered bridge in Bucks County, Pennsylvania, USA, and the restorative conference held in its wake. This emotional conference brought together the six young men who burned down the bridge with their families and members of the community. Using news footage, interviews and video of the actual conference, the documentary tells the story of a community moving through grief and anger to healing.

Family Voices

18 minutes

A documentary about family group decision making (FGDM), a restorative approach to problem solving used worldwide, in child welfare, youth justice and other situations. The film follows nine culturally, economically and geographically diverse American families on their journey of discovery of FGDM, from their initial fears, questions and hopes to their joy in seeing the process work. Children to grandparents offer their opinions and explain the FGDM process.

Facing the Demons

60 minutes

An award-winning documentary about the journey of the family and friends of murdered victim Michael Marslew, confronting face-to-face in a conference two of the offenders responsible for Michael's death. *Facing the Demons* originally aired on the ABC, Australia's public television network.

Other Resources

IIRP Globe Talking Piece

This small, squeezable ball is perfect as a talking piece for restorative circles.

Restorative Questions Cards

These handy two-sided coated 2" x 3.5" cards (pack of 100) put the essential restorative questions at your fingertips. One side has questions used to respond to challenging behavior, the other has questions to help those harmed by others' actions. The cards fit easily in a wallet.

Restorative Questions Poster

This 18" x 24" poster, designed for use in classrooms or hallways, prominently displays the essential restorative questions for easy reference in the event of a conflict or harmful incident.

About the IIRP

The International Institute for Restorative Practices (IIRP) is the world's first graduate school wholly dedicated to the emerging field of restorative practices. The IIRP is engaged in the advanced education of professionals at the graduate level and to the conduct of research that can develop the growing field of restorative practices, with the goal of positively influencing human behavior and strengthening civil society.

The Graduate School offers flexible master's degree and certificate options through a mix of hybrid and online graduate courses, independent study and professional development events held around the world. Students may complete a graduate program with little or no travel required to the IIRP campus in Bethlehem, Pennsylvania.

As the world's leading provider of restorative practices education, the IIRP has delivered professional development for tens of thousands of individuals from more than 55 countries working in education, criminal justice, and social and human services. To learn more about the IIRP Graduate School, go to **www.iirp.edu**.

Restorative Works
learning network

Restorative Works — a project of the Restorative Practices Foundation, in collaboration with the International Institute for Restorative Practices Graduate School — offers free educational content, news and announcements to help people become more knowledgeable and proficient in restorative practices.

Sign up for the Restorative Practices eForum,
the voice of Restorative Works, to receive email updates.

restorativeworks.net

About the Authors

Bob Costello is assistant commissioner for training and organizational development at the New York City Department of Probation and was formerly director of the IIRP's Training and Consulting Division. He has more than 20 years of experience in the fields of mental health, drug and alcohol rehabilitation, inpatient and outpatient services and alternative education. He has brought restorative practices training to professionals across the United States and the world in education, law enforcement and criminal justice, counseling and social work, business and other areas. He has appeared on radio numerous times as a spokesperson for restorative practices and restorative justice, most notably on the acclaimed National Public Radio program "Justice Talking."

Joshua Wachtel is the son of IIRP founding president Ted Wachtel and Community Service Foundation and Buxmont Academy (CSF Buxmont) co-founder Susan Wachtel. He attended a CSF Buxmont alternative school as a senior in high school and taught history and music at CSF Buxmont for four years. He currently resides in western Massachusetts and contributes regularly to the Restorative Practices eForum.

Ted Wachtel is the president and founder of the International Institute for Restorative Practices (iirp.edu), an accredited master's degree-granting graduate school. Wachtel and his wife, Susan, also founded the Community Service Foundation and Buxmont Academy (csfbuxmont.org), which operate schools, counseling and residential programs in Pennsylvania, employing restorative practices with delinquent and at-risk youth. Wachtel has written and produced numerous books and films on restorative practices and other topics. He has done keynote presentations and workshops on restorative justice and restorative practices at conferences and events around the world.